Robert Louis Kemp

Enoch, What Does Heaven Look Like?

Enoch's Revelation of God's Creation
Of The Universe

**Enoch's Amazing Description of His
Trip through the Heavens and to the
Throne of God**

Flying Car Publishing Company

Long Beach, California

For information, address:

Flying Car Publishing Company: First edition – July 2011
Flying Car Publishing Company
P.O. Box 91861
Long Beach, CA 90809
310-720-3703

Library of Congress Cataloging-in-Publication Data

Robert L. Kemp, 2011-
        Enoch, What Does Heaven Look Like? / Robert
                L. Kemp 1st edition
        p. cm.
        Includes bibliographical references
        ISBN 0-9841518-3-4
        ISBN 978-0-9841518-3-7
        Copyright © July 2011

1. Heaven — Christianity. 2. Angels — Christianity. 3. Enoch — Biblical Figure. 4. Religion. 5. Spirituality.

Flying Car Publishing Books are available at special discounts for bulk purchases in the United States by corporations, institutions, and other organizations. For more information, contact:

Flying Car Publishing Company, P.O. Box 91861, Long Beach, CA 90809

Table of Contents

Table of Contents

1.0   Introduction

To the reader this book is based on an **adaptation** of the book of "Genesis", "Ezekiel", and "Revelation" found in the Canonized Bible. As well as an **adaptation** from the "Book of Enoch" which is an ancient Jewish religious work, ascribed to Enoch, the great-grandfather of Noah.

The "Book of Enoch" is not currently regarded as part of the Canon of Scripture as used by any contemporary Christian groups.

However to the Jews, the book of Enoch is part of the Beta Israel canon. And, the book of Enoch is regarded as canon by the Ethiopian Orthodox Church and Eritrean Orthodox Church. And furthermore the "Book of Enoch" is found in the Apocryphal texts read by many for thousands of years.

Enoch is listed in the generations of Adam. Enoch is described as Adam's great, great, great, great grandson, through Seth. For the Bible says (Genesis 5:24) that Enoch "walked with God: and he was not; for God took him."

For the Bible gives indication that Enoch was able to avoid the mortal death ascribed to Adam's and his descendants. Additionally, climbing up the generation ladder towards Adam, Enoch is the son of Jared; his father. And climbing down the generation ladder, Enoch is described as the father of Methuselah and great-grandfather of Noah (Genesis 5:22-29).

This book *"Enoch, What Does Heaven Look Like?"* is the story of Enoch's amazing journey into the heavens, where he meets with specific angels that lead him on a trip through the various dimensions of the heavens, and eventually to the Throne of God.

This book is meant to give the reader a general description of what heaven looks like from the perspective of the man who walked with God named Enoch; the great-grandfather of Noah (Genesis 5:22-29). For the Bible says (Genesis 5:24) that Enoch "walked with God: and he was not; for God took him." Enoch is listed in the Bible and the Apocryphal works.

While Enoch is in heaven he receives revelation from God and the archangels about the first seven days of God's creation of the universe; and the mysteries of the wonders of the various heavens while he visits there. This story of Enoch's epic adventure is an *adaptation* taken from the Holy Bible, and the book of Enoch, and is written in three parts.

The first part of this book is based on an *adaptation* of the Bible's book of Genesis, and is written from the perspective of Enoch's description of the revelation that he get from the Lord, regarding the first seven days of God's Genesis of creation.

The second part of this book is meant to give a general description of what heaven looks like, and is an *adaptation* based on the "Book of Enoch" and the revelation that Enoch receives from the Lord God, as the archangels lead Enoch through the various dimensions of the heavens showing him the wonders that exists there.

The third part of this book described in the last two chapters is an *adaptation* from the Bible and the "Book of Enoch" regarding the revelation that Enoch receives about the Throne of the God, and the revelation of Jesus the Christ, the Son of God, the Son of Man (Matthew 16:13-20).

The work in this book is not the original "Book of Enoch" letter by letter, but is an *adaptation* taken from the "Book of Enoch" and the Holy Bible.

This book is written in story form and is also a form of poetry; and is not meant to be considered the cannon of Holy Scripture.

This work is not meant to be considered scripture as one would interpret the Bible.

However, the author of this book believes that this is a work inspired by God.

I hope that reading this you get a new view of the creation of universe, the heavens, and the earth; and are inspired to study the scriptures ordained in the Holy Bible.

1.1   God tells the Creation Story to Enoch

In the beginning of the days of man on earth, God created a special garden in the earth. And in that garden, He planted Homo sapiens, a mankind whose purpose was to house the Spirit and the Breath of the living God.

The linage and generations that was to come of this mankind would have the Spirit of the Living God residing within them as they walked, having dominion throughout the whole of the earth.

This is the lineage of the generation of those men from Adam to Enoch. For God the Father created the first man and named him Adam. And Adam was the father of Seth. And Seth was the father of Enosh. And Enosh was the father of Kenan. And Kenan was the father of Mahalalel. And Mahalalel was the father of Jared. And Jared, he was the father of Enoch.

Now, Enoch, the son of Jared, had the testimony; that as a man he was good and honorable, as he walked in the earth. And, Enoch was a man who sought after, and walked with God, obeying His statutes and precepts, and teaching his family and household about the Lord, continuously.

One day, the Lord God, the creator of the Heavens and the Earth being pleased with Enoch, summoned him into Heaven, for he was to receive revelation and knowledge of the creation and heavenly things; which no other man had complete knowledge of before that time.

Enoch, What Does Heaven Look Like?

And while in heaven I Enoch was commanded, to write down all that I saw, and heard. And these are the words that I was commanded to write concerning the revelation of the creation of the universe, the ten dimensions of the heavens, and the earth.

And I Enoch was walking with God along the banks of Euphrates River, when I took rest beneath a large tree. When all of a sudden, I was caught up in a vision, and as I looked, a stormy wind came out of the north, a great cloud with brightness around it and fire flashing forth continually, and in the middle of the fire, I could see something like gleaming amber.

And when I could finally, see its appearance more clearly, it reminded me of a great circle, and it was wheel shaped, and it looked like a living chariot. And I could see four living creatures around it, with four different faces. As for the appearance of the four faces of the living creatures; the face of a human being, the face of a lion on the right side, the face of a bull on the left side, and the face of an eagle.

And I Enoch was caught up in a vision, and into this living creature with the four faces, and I was summoned by the Lord of Glory into the "Tenth Dimension of Heaven", which is called "The Holy of Holies."

There, I saw the appearance of the Lord's face, like iron made to glow in fire, and from Him brought out, emitting sparks, of fire that burns.

Thus I saw the Throne of Glory and the Lord's face, but the Lord's face is ineffable, marvelous, beautiful, and very awful, and very, very terrible.

And who am I to tell of the Lord's unspeakable being, and of his very wonderful face?

The Lord's throne is very great and not made with hands. And I cannot tell the quantity of his many instructions, and various voices, or the quantity of those standing round him.

Nor, can I tell the quantity, of troops of cherubim and seraphim, nor their incessant singing, nor his immutable beauty, and who shall tell of the ineffable greatness of his glory?

And I fell prone and bowed down to the Lord, and the Lord with his lips said to me:

> "Have courage, Enoch, do not fear,
> arise and stand before my face into
> eternity and life everlasting."

And one of the Lord's archangel whose name is Michael lifted me up, and led me into the presence and before the Lord's face.

And the Lord, said to his innumerous glorious servants, tempting them:

> "Let Enoch stand before my face into
> eternity and life everlasting."

And the glorious ones round about his throne bowed down to the Lord. And they all with one voice said:

> "Let Enoch go according to Thy word."

And the Lord God said to Michael the archangel:

"Go and take Enoch from out his earthly garments, and anoint him with my sweet ointment, and put him into the garments of My Glory."

And, Michael did as the Lord commanded him. He anointed me, and dressed me in godly apparel. And my appearance was that of a great light, and the aroma of that ointment that was upon me, is like sweet hyacinth in the morning dew, and its smell pleasant and mild.

And I was shining like the sun's ray, and I looked at myself, and was like one of his glorious ones round about His Throne.

And the Lord summoned another one of his archangels who goes by the name Pravuil, whose knowledge was quicker in wisdom than the other archangels, who wrote all the deeds of the Lord; and the Lord said to Pravuil:

"Bring out the books from my store-houses, and provide a writing utensil, and give it to Enoch, and deliver to him the choice and comforting books which are in thy hand."

And I Enoch was caught up in a vision, and I was before the great Throne of the Lord and I did hear secrets from God; which God revealed to me, and spoke with me face to face.

And the Lord summoned me, and said:

> *"Enoch, sit down on my left with Gabriel".*

And I, Enoch bowed down to the Lord, and the Lord spoke to me saying:

> *"Enoch, beloved, all that you see, all things that are standing finished, I will tell you how they were created; even before the very beginning of the foundations of the universe, all that I created from non-being, and the visible things which came forth from the invisible."*

> *"Hear, Enoch, and take in these my words, for not to My angels have I told my secrets, and I have not told them their rise, nor my endless realm, nor have they understood all of my creation, which I will tell you today."*

Even as one of the archangels Gabriel which stood on the left side of God, he heard not the words which the Lord spoke only to me, Enoch, face to face, saying:

> *"In the beginning, before all things were visible, I alone used to go about in the invisible things. Like the sun from east to west, and from west to east; went I up and down in the invisible."*

> *"And while I was walking up and down in the invisible, I conceived the thoughts of*

placing the foundations of the heavens and the earth, and of creating the visible things of the universe."

Surprisingly, I could comprehend what the Lord explained to me, about His creation; and how He decided all measure and portion, by his wisdom, of the visible and the invisible. From the invisible He made all things visible, Himself being invisible.

And I, Enoch could hear and understand the Lord's thoughts by his Spirit, and my heart, mind and soul was enriched at the hearing of God describing, how out of the very lowest darkness comes down the visible from the invisible.

And I heard the Lord God say:

> *"In the beginning the universe was without form, and void; and there was darkness everywhere. And the Spirit of God moved upon the darkness at My command creating the heavens and the earth."*

> *"I commanded in the very lowest parts, that visible things should come forth from the invisible."*

> *"Then, I the Lord said: 'Let there be Light'"*

> *"And at my command "Adoil" came out very great, and I beheld him, and lo! He had a belly of great light."*

"And I said to him: 'Become undone, Adoil, and let the visible come out of you.'"

"And he came undone, and a great light came out. And I was in the midst of that great light. And as there is born light from light, there came forth a great age, and revealed all creation, which I had thought to create."

And I, Enoch by the spirit was able to understand, that God called "Light" out of "Darkness." And this is a very great mystery!

While I was in heaven God showed unto me, Enoch, all his wisdom and power, throughout the time, which I spent in heaven. He revealed how he created all the heavenly and earthly forces and all moving things, even down to man. And, I wrote down all that I was commanded, saw, and heard.

1.2 The First (1st) Day of Creation

I, Enoch was summoned into Heaven and it was revealed to me the joys of the Lord's creation, and about its "First Day"; and how He worked on that day to bound and set limits on His handy work.

God conveyed to me, Enoch, that "Adoil the Light", pleased God so much because it obeyed his commands, and loved to be around him and wrapped itself around him like a garment, and begged not to be disrobed; and announced continuous loyalty and service at His commands.

This "Adoil the Light" pleased the lord so much that He built his surroundings out of its essence. And the Lord said unto me:

> "And I the Lord said; Let there be 'Light'; and there was light and a 'Cosmic Force.' And I the Lord God divided the light from the darkness."

> "And I saw the "Light" that it was good."

> "And I placed for myself a Throne, and took my seat upon it, and said to the light:"

> "Go up higher and fix yourself high above the throne, and be a foundation to the highest things."

> "And above the light there is nothing else, and then I the Lord, bent up and

looked up from my Throne, and there was a beautiful rainbow; and I was well pleased with the light."

And, it was revealed to me, Enoch, that the Lord was so pleased by the obedience of "Light" that he made for him a companion, and set a place for it to rest when it wants to rest from its unceasing and continuous loyalty and service to God.

Likewise, it was revealed to me, Enoch, that the companion of this "Adoil" which is light is called "Archas"; and is matter. This companion of "Adoil the Light" is "Archas the Matter" which appears in two forms, one form is visible and the other form is invisible.

Then, God summons from the very lowest a second time that "Archas", very energetic and heavy should come forth. And the Lord said:

"I commanded in the very lowest parts, a second time that visible things should come forth from the invisible."

"Then, I the Lord said: 'Let "Archas" come forth hard and let there be Matter.'"

"And at my command "Archas" came forth, hard, heavy, and very energetic, from the invisible. And, I beheld him, and lo! He would be the tangible of visible and invisible things in the universe."

The First (1st) Day of Creation

"And I the Lord said:

"Be opened, Archas, and let there be born from you tangible things, and he came undone. And an age of matter came forth, very great and very dark, bearing the creation of all lower things."

"And I the Lord saw that it was good and said to him:"

"Archas go down below, and make yourself firm and be a firmament, and be for a foundation for the lower things."

"And at My command he went down and fixed himself, and became the foundation for the lower things, and below the darkness there is nothing else."

"Then I the Lord, bent down and looked down from my Throne, and there was a foundation to create tangible things; and I was well pleased with the matter."

Then the Lord conveyed to me, Enoch that He created another material in the universe, that has a spiritual essence; and it flows and He called its name "water."

And the Lord revealed to me that this water is made of light and matter, and He established the water in the different dimensions of the heavens and the earth.

The First (1st) Day of Creation

And the Lord said:

> *"And I commanded that the spiritual essence of the water should be taken from light and from darkness."*

> *"And I the Lord said to the water: 'Be thick and flow' and it became as I commanded.'"*

> *"And I spread out the thick flowing substance between the light and the darkness, and it became water, and I spread it out over the darkness, below the light, in the firmament of the heavens."*

It was therefore revealed, that water has a spiritual essence and was made of a mixing of matter and light. I was amazed at the creative power of God, as I envisioned Him stirring this mixture creating visible from the invisible like a potter at his wheel.

And thus, I heard the Lord say:

> *"And then I made firm the waters; that is to say, I separated the waters above from the waters beneath; and set the bottomless firm."*

> *"And I made firm the foundation of light and darkness, and in between the waters, were heavenly dimensions from inside, and outside; and I imaged it like crystal wet and dry, that is to say like glass."*

Enoch, What Does Heaven Look Like?

The First (1st) Day of Creation

"And I circumvented the waters and the heavenly dimensions, and other elements. And then I made firm the heavenly circles, and made the lower water which is under heaven collect itself together, into one whole; and that it would be separated from the upper water which is above the heaven to collect itself together, into one whole."

"And I showed each one of them its road, and the various dimensions of the heavens and the earth, each one of them in its heaven, that they go where I commanded."

"And I saw that it was good."

"And I separated between light and between darkness that is to say in the midst of the water that it should go here and that it should go there."

"And I said to the light, that it should be the day. And to the darkness, that it should be the night."

*"And there was evening and there was **morning the first day**; all of this I did in the time span of approximately two billion years."*

And, I Enoch wrote down all that I was commanded, saw, and heard.

Enoch, What Does Heaven Look Like?

1.3   The Second (2nd) Day of Creation

I, Enoch was summoned into Heaven and it was revealed to me the joys of the Lord's creation, and about its "Second Day." The second day is called the fiery Essence. For on that day, God finished the framework of the dimensions of the heavens. And afterward He fashioned the angelic beings and heavenly troops.

And as I Enoch was contemplating what God did on the "First Day", creating light, darkness, and the material for heavenly dimensions, that I heard the Lord say:

> *"And after the "First Day" I the Lord said, Let there be a firmament in the midst of the expanding heavenly dimensions of the waters, and let it divide the 'Hot Dark Matter' from the 'Cold Dark Matter'."*

> *"And I the Lord God made the firmament grid which is the structure of space and time, waves, and fields of the universe. And I divided the matter which was internal to the firmament from the matter which was external to the firmament: and it was so."*

> *"And I saw the structure of the universe and the dimensions of the heavens emerge according to My command, and I was pleased, and it was good!"*

Thus it was explained to me, Enoch that God made the firmament grid which is the space and time, and divided the waters which were under the firmament from the waters which were above the firmament. And these He called the dimensions of the heavens of the Universe. And the constituents of the heavens rotated.

And as I was pondering on the wonders of the "Second Day" of the Lord's magnificent creation; that it was later revealed to me that during that second day the Lord was also at work creating angelic beings.

And I Enoch heard the Lord say:

> *"And I the Lord God imagined that there should be workers in this heaven to monitor and attend to all created things. And I decided for all different choirs, orders, and ranks of the heavenly angelic troops."*

> *"And, I imagined the image and essence of fire, and my eye looked at the very hard, firm rock, and from the gleam of my eye the lightning received its wonderful nature. And I could see a rock, fire, and water as one. And this rock which is both fire and water and water and fire; and one does not put out the other, nor does the one dry up the other."*

> *"Therefore I decided that the heavenly beings would be as bright as the*

lightning is brighter than the sun, softer than water and firmer than hard rock."

"And from the rock I cut off a great fire. And from the fire I created the choirs, orders, and ranks of the incorporeal troops. I created a great variety of many troops of angelic beings."

"And after I finished creating the innumerous incorporeal angelic beings. I numbered them all and fixed that number; and from that point forward, I created not one more angel after that number was fixed."

"And their essences are fiery and their raiment a burning flame. And I commanded that each one should stand in his choir, order, and rank."

"And, I the Lord God that knows the beginning from the end looked forward into time, and I witnessed the future of these angelic beings."

"And one of the archangels that I spent special care designing, and whom I loved; the archangel "Lucifer"; the light bearing one; and leader of the high praise angels. He would sin!"

"And, I the Lord God that knows the beginning from the end looked forward and could see that this archangel "Lucifer" would have his name changed

to "Satan" the devil. And he with his follower angels would be thrown down from the height of heaven."

"And this "Lucifer" which became "Satan"; which is one, from out of the high praise order of angels. Lucifer having turned his heart away from Me, with a portion of the order that was under him; conceived an impossible thought."

"That he might be able to place his throne higher than the clouds above the heavens, that he might become equal in rank to the Lord God Almighty."

"I the Lord, called those thoughts and that work that Lucifer would conceive, sin."

"Then, I the Lord said: 'After sin what is there but death?' My words never return to me void. And they hasten to my command."

"Thus I the Lord was grieved at the thoughts that the archangel Lucifer, would have in the future."

"And seeing the future, although I loved "Lucifer" I knew that I would someday threw him out from the height of heaven, with his following angels, and he would fly in the air continuously above the bottomless pit."

*"And the evening and the morning were the **second day**; all of this I did in the time span of approximately two billion years."*

And, I Enoch turned to look at Gabriel standing next to me and God, as I pondered what happened in the days of Gabriel. Since Gabriel and his kind was fashioned on the "Second Day."

And I became aware that a great war in God's kingdom had taken place, all on the account of this archangel whose name was Lucifer.

As I pondered about this "war in heaven" and the great sin of disobedience that occurred by some of the angels. And about what might have happened during that time. I recalled that the sin of disobedience not only happened in heaven, but this also happened in the earth as well; like in the days of Adam disobedience.

And as I Enoch was pondering, God spoke to me saying:

> *"I will reveal what happened to your fathers and the reason the 'Son of Man' whose name is "Jesus" will come and wash away all sin from the heavens and the earth. For all sin leads to death, whether it is in heaven or in the earth."*

And, I Enoch wrote down all that I was commanded, saw, and heard.

1.4 The Third (3rd) Day of Creation

I, Enoch was summoned into Heaven and it was revealed to me the joys of the Lord's creation, and about its "Third Day." And on the "Third day" the basic properties of the dry land and the earth were designed, and created for the various dimensions of the heavens!

And I, Enoch was full of wonder and amazement as I paid close attention to what was being revealed to me, and I continued to write as I also was commanded; and thus, I heard the Lord say:

> *"And I the Lord God on the "Third Day" imagined a place for creatures to roam and to have a place for rest in the various heavens; and I said:"*

> *"'Let the waters under the heavens be gathered together unto one place, and let the dry land appear in those places; and I saw chaos become dry'; and it was so."*

> *"For, out of the waves I created the rocks hard and big, and from the rocks, I piled up the dry, and the dry I called the earth."*

> *"And I the Lord God called the dry lands that would exist in the various heavens Earth; and the gathering together of the waters within the earth the Seas."*

The Third (3rd) Day of Creation

"And I saw that it was good."

"And in the midst of the earth I called abyss, that is to say the bottomless; I collected the sea in one place and bound it together with a yoke."

"And I made commands to the sea: 'Behold I give you your eternal limits in the earth and you shall not break loose from your boundary parts.'"

"And I the Lord God said: Let the earth bring forth the condensed elements of matter, and the matter combined; and the matter became molecules, after its kind which evolved, whose self replicating properties is in itself, upon the earth: and it was so."

"And I saw the earth which brought forth an abundance of elements after its kind which evolved into: hydrogen, helium, carbon, iron, oxygen, and all sorts of solids, liquids, gases, and plasmas; and the atoms and molecules, whose self replication is within it."

"And I saw that it was good."

"And I the Lord God said: 'Let the earth bring forth grass, the herb yielding seed, and the fruit tree yielding fruit after his kind, whose seed is in itself, upon the earth'; and it was so."

Enoch, What Does Heaven Look Like?

The Third (3rd) Day of Creation

"And I saw the earth which brought forth grass and herb yielding seed after his kind, and the tree yielding fruit, whose seed was in it, after his kind."

"And I saw that it was good."

"And, on the third day I commanded the earth to make grow great and fruitful trees, and hills, and seed to sow."

"And I gathered together in divers places salt water seas, oceans, rivers, lakes, and streams"

"And I planted a garden of paradise, with two great trees in the midst, the "Tree of Life" and the "Tree of Knowledge of Good and Evil" and enclosed it; and placed as armed guardians flaming angels, to watch over it."

*"And the evening and the morning were the **third day**; all of this I did in the time span of approximately two billion years."*

It was revealed to me Enoch that on the "Third day" the basic archetype for the earth was created and placed throughout the heavens; but the earth that mankind would be planted upon was placed on the "First Heaven!

And I, Enoch was an earthly witness in the heavenly realm, and in the Throne room of the Most Holy, the Lord Most High. And I witnessed the angelic host of those standing round Him; troops of cherubim and seraphim, with their incessant singing of praise and of the greatness of His Glory. And, I wrote down all that I was commanded, saw, and heard.

1.5 The Fourth (4th) Day of Creation

I, Enoch was summoned into Heaven and it was revealed to me the joys of the Lord's creation, and about its "Fourth Day." It is on the "Fourth day" that the habitation of the earth, and the "First Heaven" was designed, to be suitable for life; and where God would ultimately place mankind.

And I, Enoch desiring to know more about God and His creating power, found myself not worthy to hear such things. And the archangel Gabriel made known unto me that the robe of Godly apparel which I wore, allowed me to be worthy to hear the Words of God. And I Enoch therefore, praised God saying:

> "Glory and Honor, and everlasting Blessing be upon He, who made the Heavens and the Earth. And all that He has made is good!"

The praise and humility of Enoch pleased God; so that He continued with His revelation to Enoch face to face.

Then the Lord said to Enoch:

> "On the "Fourth Day" I commanded that there should be great lights in the heavens; that they would give light upon the earths."

> "Likewise, on the "Fourth Day" I commanded in the "First Heaven" that there should be great lights in that

25

heaven to light a special earth. And I set them on their course that they would give light upon the earth where I would plant mankind."

"And I the Lord God said: 'Let there be galaxies, stars, planets, and moons, and let them be as lights in the firmament of the heavens; to divide the day from the night. And let them be for signs, and for seasons, for years, and days. And I set them on their courses and in their specific locations"

"And I set the galaxies, the stars, the planets, and the moons and all of the works of My imaginings of celestial bodies in motion. And I could see new births and new creations of all sorts of stars, in the stellar voids of creation."

"And let them be for lights in the firmament of the heaven to give light upon the earth where I would plant mankind; and it was so."

"And I the Lord God made two great lights to rule the earth where I would plant mankind. The greater light the sun star to rule the day, and the lesser light the moon which rules the night: I thus fixed the sun star, the solar system, the planets and the moons also."

"And I gave command that they would give light upon the earth, and to rule

over the day and over the night, and to divide the light from the darkness; and let them be for signs, and for seasons, and for years, and for months, and for days."

"The sun that it should go according to a season of twelve; and I appointed the succession of the months to its turning"

"And in the firmament of Heaven all the great celestials I gave names, and lives, their thundering, and their hour-markings, and how they should succeed; I gave a time and a season to all celestial bodies."

"And I saw that it was good."

*"And the evening and the morning were the **fourth day**; all of this I did in the time span of approximately two billion years."*

And I, Enoch began to understand that on the "Fourth Day" the Lord fashioned the right environment for man's earth to exist. It being the right distance from the sun and moon, and having an exact location in the solar system, and the galaxy.

And I began to understand that the Lord is a God of seasons, and of dates, and that the times of things in the heavenly universe were important to Him. And, I wrote down all that I was commanded, saw, and heard.

1.6 The Fifth (5ᵗʰ) Day of Creation

I, Enoch was summoned into Heaven and it was revealed to me the joys of the Lord's creation, and about its "Fifth Day." And the fifth day it was then that the Lord began to exercise His skill and understanding of genetics and to create sea and air faring biology in the Earth.

And, I, Enoch was informed that after the "Fourth Day" was completed that the earth was a suitable place for habitation. And from that day forward, the Lord moved from the creating of the mechanics of the heavens, the stars, and the earth, that He, began to focus on earthly sea and air faring "Genetics" and "Biology."

And the Lord commanded me Enoch to pay close attention and He said:

> *"On the fifth day I commanded the sea that it should bring forth abundantly the moving creature that has life, and fowl that may fly above the earth in the open firmament of heaven."*

> *"And I the Lord created whales, fishes, sea creatures, and feathered birds of many sizes and varieties, abundantly. And I created every living creature that moves, which the waters brought forth abundantly, after their kind, and every winged fowl after his kind."*

"The creatures large and small that I made which originated in the sea began to multiply, each species evolving in separate boundaries after its kind; the sea animals after its kind and the foul after its kind."

"And I gave them choices some remained in the sea, some came out of the sea upon the land, and, some went gladly into the air."

"And I said to them with joy and gladness be blessed to dwell in the earth. Enjoy its tasty fruits, smell the savor of the air, multiply, and fill the waters and the seas. And let the fowl soar through the air flapping with wings continuously rejoicing in the wondrous earthly habitation"

"And I saw that it was good."

"And I the Lord God blessed them, saying; 'Be fruitful, and multiply, and evolve, and fill the waters in the seas, and fill the air soaring with winds in your wings; and let all the sea and air faring creatures multiply evolving in the earth."

*"And the evening and the morning were the **fifth day**; all of this I did in the time span of approximately two billion years."*

And I, Enoch began to understand that all the sea and air faring creatures in the earth were the result of the

Lord's biological and genetic omniscience. And, I wrote down all that I was commanded, saw, and heard.

1.7   *The Sixth (6th) Day of Creation*

I, Enoch was summoned into Heaven and it was revealed to me the joys of the Lord's creation, and about its "Sixth Day." And the sixth day it was then that the Lord began to exercise His skill and understanding of genetics and to create land faring biology in the Earth.

And, I, Enoch was informed that after the "Fifth Day" was completed that the Lord moved on, from creating earthly sea and air faring genetics and biology, that He began to focus on earthly land faring genetics" and biology.

And the Lord commanded me once again to pay very close attention and He said:

> *"And I the God said: Let the earth bring forth the living land creatures which would evolve after his kind."*

> *"And I created the mammals, reptiles, and cattle to evolve after its kind, and I created the creeping thing and bugs of all sorts after its kind; and the various large and small beast of the earth after his kind: and it was so."*

> *"And I saw that it was good."*

> *"And I the Lord God created lesser and greater hominids which would evolve after his kind. The greater hominids I*

called man after the image, of my likeness."

"And I the Lord God commanded that the greater hominids would walk standing upright in the earth and that they would have dominion over the fish of the sea, and over the fowl of the air, and over the cattle, and over all the earth, and over every creeping thing that creeps upon the earth.

"So, I the Lord God created hominid man so that he would evolve into the true image of God, I created he him; male and female I created them."

"And I the Lord God blessed them, and said unto them, be fruitful, and multiply, and replenish the earth, and subdue it: and have dominion over the fish of the sea, and over the fowl of the air, and over every living thing that moves upon the earth."

"And I the Lord God said: 'Behold, I have given you every herb bearing seed, which is upon the face of all the earth, and every tree, in which is the fruit of a tree yielding seed; to you it shall be for meat."

"And to every beast of the earth, and to every fowl of the air, and to everything that creeps upon the earth, wherein

there is life, I have given every green herb for meat: and it was so."

"And I saw that it was good."

*"And the evening and the morning were the **sixth day**; all of this I did in the time span of approximately two billion years."*

And I, Enoch began to understand that all the land faring creatures and the hominid man in the earth were the result of the Lord's biological and genetic omniscience. And, I wrote down all that I was commanded, saw, and heard.

1.8   The Seventh (7th) Day of Creation

I, Enoch was summoned into Heaven and it was revealed to me the joys of the Lord's creation, and about its "Seventh Day." And the seventh day is known as the day of rest, because it is that day that the Lord rested from his six days of labor creating the heavens and the earth.

And, I, Enoch rejoiced with the Lord and the angels, at the understanding, that what God starts He also finishes!

Then the Lord said to me:

> *"I am the Lord God that creates all things for my good pleasure; and after creating for six days, the heavens and the earth were finished, and all the host of them was also completed."*

> *"And on the beginning of the seventh day, I contemplated all the work which I had created; and thus I rested on the seventh day; from six days of work on the heavens and the earth which I had made."*

> *"And I the Lord God blessed the seventh day, and sanctified it; because I was pleased with all my work in the completing, and the efficiency of it; Therefore, I rested from all the work which I the Lord created and made."*

The Seventh (7th) Day of Creation

*"And the evening and the morning of the day of rest were the **seventh day**; all of this I did in the time span of approximately two billion years."*

"Then, I the Lord God at the end of the seventh day had a similar thought, like I had on the second day, when I decided to create the innumerous incorporeal angelic beings to attend and work the heavens."

"So I thought to create a spirit man being which would be separate and different in likeness and essence from the angelic beings. For this man would be created to walk upon, to work, and to rule in the earth."

"And I communed with my Father self, my Holy Spirit self, and my Wisdom Word self, which is the Son of God."

"Then I said: 'Let us make man in our image, after our likeness.'"

"And in the image of God did I create a "Spirit Man" being, which is separate and different in essence from the angelic beings."

"And I the Lord commanded that this man would house the Spirit and Breath of God. And he would have dominion in the earth and over the fish of the sea, and over the fowl of the air, and over the

Enoch, What Does Heaven Look Like?

cattle, and over all the earth, and over every creeping thing that creeps upon the earth."

"So I the Lord God created a "Spirit Man" in my own image, in the image of God, I created he him; male and female I created them."

"Then I the Lord God fashioned a fleshly body for the man, from the dust of the earth. I shaped him, and formed a fleshly image from the earth that I would take pleasure in the residence of My Breath and Spirit."

"And I Lord God formed man from the dust of the earthly ground, and breathed into his nostrils the breath of life; and the "Spirit Man" that became flesh became a living soul."

"Then, I commanded the Wisdom Word to create in the flesh of man seven unique consistencies:"

"And the Wisdom Word created life in his blood; his eyes; his bones, his intelligence, his veins, his hair; and his soul from my Breath and Spirit."

"And I commanded that the Wisdom Word would create in his flesh seven unique sensing natures. And the Wisdom Word created his hearing,

sight, smell, touch, taste, endurance, and intelligence."

"And I the Lord was so pleased with the finished creation of man that I said: 'I created the nature of man from the invisible, and from a visible earthly nature; he has life, breath, and a Godly image; he knows speech like some created thing; he is small in greatness, and again, he is great in smallness.'"

"And I presented the created spirit-man of flesh, to the angels in heaven; so that they would adore and rejoice with me at my creation. That they also would rejoice about the man that I created that has flesh, spirit, and soul."

"Then did Heaven and the angels rejoice with me and my creation; but there were some angels that did not rejoice."

"And I did nothing about those that did not rejoice; for I knew that there would be at the end of time and at the 'Day of Judgment' those disobedient angelic ones will be judged by the man for whom they would not bow."

"And I placed man on earth, as a second angel, honorable, great and glorious, and full of my Spirit."

"And I appointed the man as ruler, to rule upon the earth and to have my wisdom, for he was created by the Wisdom Word that Son of God."

"And there was none like him upon the earth or in heaven of all my existing creatures."

"And I appointed him a name, from the four component parts of the earth, from east, from west, from south, from north, and I called his name Adam."

"And I showed the man Adam the ways of the light and the darkness. And I instructed him by saying: 'This is good, and that is bad.'"

"When I created the man, I gave the man Adam a free will, that I should learn whether he has love towards me, or hatred; that it be clear whether he loves me or not."

"And, I the Lord God that knows the beginning from the end looked forward into time, and I witnessed the future of this mankind."

"I, the Lord God have seen the future and his nature, but he has not seen his own nature; and because he sees not himself he will sin worse."

The Seventh (7th) Day of Creation

"And I the Lord said: 'After sin what is there but death?' My words never return to me void. And they hasten to my command"

"And I the Lord God planted a special garden in the earth that I named Eden. And in eastward of the garden in Eden there I put the man whom I had formed, to attend it and to maintain it."

"Out of the ground of Eden I made to grow every tree that is pleasant to the sight, and good for food."

"I planted two beautiful and special trees in the midst of the garden: the "Tree of Life" and the "Tree of Knowledge of Good and Evil."

"And I the Lord God commanded the man Adam, saying: 'Of every tree of the garden you mat freely eat, but of the "Tree of Life" you shall not eat of it. And more especially you are directly commanded not to eat of the "Tree of Knowledge of Good and Evil"; you shall never ever eat of it. For in the day that you eat of that tree you shall surely die.'"

"I made a river to flow out of Eden to water the garden, where I put the man and the special trees. And from that location the river divides and becomes four branches. The name of the first river is Pishon; the second river is

Gihon; the third river is Tigris, and the fourth river is the Euphrates."

"And I the Lord God brought every beast of the field, and every fowl of the air that goes about in the earth, and presented them unto the man Adam, to see what he would name them. And whatsoever Adam called every living creature that was presented to him, that was the name of that creature unto this day. And Adam gave names to all cattle, and to the fowl of the air, and to every beast of the field that goes about in the earth."

"And after I spent a very long time alone educating and communing with the man Adam, I decided that it is not good that the male should be alone. And I decided that I would make for him a female companion, a help meet for him. And she would be called his wife."

"Thus, I put to sleep the male, Adam, and he fell asleep. And I took from him a rib, and created a female which emerged as a man with a womb. And she would be called his wife."

"And when the man Adam was awakened from his sleep, I presented unto the man Adam the female that I created from his own flesh."

"And the man Adam was so very pleased with the female that he saw that

his face lighted up like the sun, and he had a smile from ear to ear the size of a rainbow. And being very delighted with the woman that he saw that he began to prophesy and said, 'this is now bone of my bones, and flesh of my flesh, she shall be called "Woman", because she was taken out of Man. Therefore shall a man leave his father and his mother, and shall cleave unto his wife: and the two of them shall be one flesh."

"And Adam had earlier learned to name all of the creatures that I the Lord would present to him; therefore he named his wife, Eve. And they were both naked in the garden, the man Adam and his wife Eve; and they were not ashamed."

"And I blessed them, and said unto them, be fruitful, and multiply, and replenish the earth, and subdue it: and have dominion over the fish of the sea, and over the fowl of the air, and over every living thing that moves upon the earth."

"And I said, Behold, I have given you every herb bearing seed, which is upon the face of all the earth, and every tree, in which is the fruit of a tree yielding seed; to you it shall be for meat."

"And to every beast of the earth, and to every fowl of the air, and to everything that creeps upon the earth, wherein

there is life, I have given every green herb for meat: and it was so."

"And I looked back and considered all of my creation and everything that I had made; and that it was very good."

And I, Enoch began to understand that although the "Seventh Day" is known as the day of rest, because it is that day that the Lord rested from his six days of work, creating the heavens and the earth.

However, soon afterward on the "Eight Day" He went right back to work, in the earth, and made a special garden, there He created and planted, our father Adam, and the mother Eve; the parents of all mankind that houses the Breath and Spirit of the Lord Almighty. And I, Enoch wrote down all that I was commanded, saw, and heard.

1.9 The Fall of Man and the Earthly Creation

I Enoch was summoned into the presence of God and before the heavenly host of angels, where it was revealed to me that when God finished the creation of the man Adam, that He was very happy and full of joy; because He created a highly favored created being that would be host to His Breath and Spirit.

And it was explained to me that the Lord presented the man Adam, as highly favored to the angels in heaven with joy and gladness.

And that the Lord God informed the angels that this human being is highly favored above all creatures that He made; and although the man was formed after them, the man creature, was chosen to be above them. And God informed the angels that they would be servants unto the descendents of this human being known as the man, Adam.

However, not long after the joy and elation that God experienced because of His creation, the man Adam; that the man Adam became disobedient to the commandment of God, and God went from joy to disappointment. For the highly favored man Adam had been led into the sin of disobedience.

And the Lord said unto me Enoch:

> *"To the man Adam I gave life on earth, and I created a special garden in the east of Eden, that he should observe and keep my commands."*

"I made the heavens open to him, that he should see the angels in heaven singing the songs of victory, and witnessing the glorious light."

"And I put the man Adam continuously in a perpetual paradise, that even death has no hold on him."

"Then that Satan, whom I cast out from heaven, throwing him down to the ground, he seeing the man Adam in paradise, became extremely jealous and envious.

"For that Satan, understood that I created a wonderful habitation world for Adam to live. And because I loved the man Adam greatly, I made him lord on earth, to rule it, and to subdue it."

And, it was revealed to me Enoch that during the "Sixth Day" of creation, that Lucifer the high praise archangel became aware of God's plans to create a man creature that would be raised to a rank higher than the angels, that Lucifer started a revolt and created a war in heaven; before he was eventually thrown out of heaven.

And the day that Lucifer was thrown down from heaven light lightning, that his name was changed from Lucifer to Satan also known as the devil. The devil is the evil spirit of the lower places of heaven and earth. And as a fugitive he made the choice to make war in heaven, from the heavens, and in the earth; and his name was changed to Satan.

This archangel Lucifer his heart was changed and he became different from the angels, because of his rebellion and disobedience. As listed with Lucifer's rebellion and disobedience he was able to convince one third of the angels to follow him in this rebellion and revolt; turning the hearts of the angels away from the Lord Almighty.

However; when Lucifer the Satan and his compatriot angels were thrown down from heaven; his intelligence as far as his understanding of righteous and sinful things remained.

Now, after the Lord cast out Lucifer and the angels, there was no bottomless pit reserved for them yet. Therefore, the Lord God the creator of the heavens and the earth changed the design of the "Second Heaven" from a beautiful place, to be a desolate place that would be suitable to chain Satan and the fallen angels.

So during this time when the "Second Heaven" was being redesigned from being beautiful to being desolate; Satan and the fallen angels were able to roam free through the lower heavens and the earth until they would be placed in captivity.

And Satan the devil being free to roam the lower places of the heavens understood his own condemnation and the sin which he had sinned before, he was thrown down. Thus, Satan the devil therefore conceived thought against God's highly favored creature, the man, Adam; that he would turn the man's heart away from God.

Therefore, Satan the devil sought to destroy Adam for the love that God showed to him, and the perpetual state of joy that God had given unto man in the garden. Thus, he was exceedingly jealous.

Therefore, Satan the devil conceived in his heart that if he could get the man to sin before the Lord; that God would throw the man down from his elevated position of first rank among his creatures. Satan the devil thought that God would be so angry with the man because of sin, that He would once again restore the angels to the position of first rank among all creatures.

Then, Satan the devil devised a plan that he would transform in a great apparition enter the eastward in the Garden of Eden, and cause Adam and Eve to sin. As part of his evil plan the devil realized through deception and lying, that he could enter one of the creatures that roamed the garden in which he could seduce and beguile Eve.

For, Satan the devil knew that it would be exceedingly difficult to get to the heart and mind of the man Adam; and that he would not be able to convince Adam to sin. For, God spent a long time alone, educating and communing with the man Adam, instructing him about what was good and what was bad.

Now, Satan that devil devised a plan to transform into one of the creatures in the garden. And Satan tried every creature in the garden but none would receive him except for the serpent. The serpent without reservation agreed to accept the spirit of the devil and the serpent gave the devil access to the man Adam and Eve in the garden.

Now the serpent was more subtil than any beast of the field which the Lord God had made. So slight and crafty was the serpent that it was difficult for Adam or Eve to detect that it was actually the devil.

And Satan in the form of the snake said to the woman:

> "Is it really true that God has said that you shall not eat of every tree of the garden?"

And the woman said unto the serpent:

> "God has said that we may eat of all the fruit of the trees of the garden, but of the fruit of the tree which is in the midst of the garden, God has said, that we shall not eat of it, neither shall you touch it; and the day that you do, you will surely die."

And the serpent with the intention of beguiling her said unto the woman:

> "Did God really say that fruit of the tree in the midst of the garden is forbidden fruit?"

> "For, if you eat of the tree in the midst of the garden, you shall not surely die. For God does know that in the day that you eat of that tree, then your eyes shall be opened, and you shall be as gods, knowing good and evil; and you will be like He is!"

47

And, when the woman Eve, being convinced by the snake the it would be safe to eat of the tree that God had commanded them not the eat. For the serpent had turned the heart and the mind of the woman Eve, to question the intentions of God. And she began to think that God was in some way keeping something good back from them, by telling them not to eat of the trees in the midst of the garden.

Now, after the woman Eve, was convinced by the devil that she would not die, if she ate of the tree that God commanded them not to eat. She saw that the tree was good for food, and that it was pleasant to the eyes, and a tree to be desired to make one wise.

Then the woman Eve, took of the fruit from the "Tree of Knowledge of Good and Evil", and did eat!

And, after the woman Eve did eat of the forbidden fruit, she afterwards did look for her husband, and presented the fruit, convincing the man that by eating the forbidden fruit it was really good to eat, and to the taste, and that they would not die. And she gave the forbidden fruit also unto her husband to eat with her.

And the man Adam also did eat of the forbidden fruit. And the eyes of them both were opened, and they knew that they were naked; and they sewed fig leaves together, and made themselves aprons.

Now, it was revealed to me Enoch that the man Adam did eat of the fruit of the tree disobeying God and did sin. But Adam's sin against God was not that of lust for power, and the desire to become as wise as a god; being deceived of the Devil.

The man Adam sinned before the face of the Lord because of his love for his wife Eve.

The woman Eve sinned before the face of the Lord because of lust for power, and the desire to become as wise as a god; and she was deceived of the devil, not the man Adam.

Now this is what really happened, after Eve ate of the forbidden fruit of the tree in the midst of the garden, she sought for her husband that he too should eat. And, Adam said to his wife Eve:

> "My beloved Eve, what have you done? God commanded that we should not eat of that tree in the midst of the garden. And He said that if we do eat of it, we shall surely die."

Then Eve said to her husband Adam:

> "My husband, the serpent in the midst of the garden said to me, 'You shall not surely die, but when you eat your eyes will be opened and that I would be as wise as a god."

> "Look, my husband, I did eat, and I am not dead, and my eyes have become enlightened."

Then Adam, said to Eve:

> "Woman, you are a fool! I have walked with God, and He does not lie. He will surely destroy you. And He will take you

from me and utterly destroy you! And I will be alone in this garden again!"

Then Adam which not having eaten of the forbidden fruit that his Wife Eve presented to him yet! Was exceedingly grieved in his heart, at what Eve had done eating from the tree that God commanded them not to eat from.

And as the man Adam pondered within his heart and mind, the actions that God might take on the woman Eve, based on His commandment; that in the day that they ate of the tree, they would surely die. Adam was so overwhelmed with the contemplation of God's punishment that he began to sweat drops of blood from his forehead.

And it entered into Adam's remembrance the amount of time that he spent in the garden alone; without Eve. And the man Adam imagined that God would destroy Eve, and take her from him; and he would be alone again.

And with the thought of God killing Eve and taking her away from him that the man Adam came to the conclusion in his heart, and in his mind, that he would not be able to endure life in the earth without his beloved wife Eve.

After much anguish and debate in his mind, and because the man Adam had great and exceeding love for his wife Eve; that he did take the fruit into his hands, and did eat of the forbidden fruit with her.

And Adam said to his wife Eve.

"Woman, you are a fool! But I love you so much because you are the bone of my bones, and flesh of my flesh; and I would not be able to live another day in the earth without you in my presence."

"For since the day that the Lord presented you to me, I have loved you. And I believe for your disobedience God will surely and utterly destroy you and take you from me."

"And if you die, then I too will die. Give me also the fruit to eat!"

So, Adam with his wife Eve did eat of the forbidden fruit, and both he and his wife's eyes were opened and they both became aware of good and evil. And they knew that they were naked; and they sewed fig leaves together, and made themselves aprons.

And soon afterwards they heard the voice of the LORD God walking in the garden in the cool of the day. And Adam and his wife hid themselves from the presence of the LORD God among the trees of the garden.

And the LORD God called unto Adam, and said unto him:

> *"Adam, where are you? Adam where are you, I love you!"*

And the LORD God called unto Adam, a second time, and said unto him:

"Adam, where are you? Adam where are you, I love you!"

For, at all other times when Adam and Eve would hear God walking in the garden, in the cool of the day, they would come running up to him with joy and adoration, to see him; similar to a pet that is overjoyed when it sees that their master has come home.

And Adam said to the Lord:

> "I heard your voice in the garden, and I was afraid, because I was naked; and I hid myself."

And the LORD said unto Adam:

> *"Who told you that you were naked? Have you eaten of the tree, where I commanded that you should not eat?"*

And the man Adam said to the Lord:

> "The woman that you presented and gave to be with me, she gave me of the tree, and I did eat."

And the LORD said unto the woman Eve:

> *"What is this that you have done?"*

And the woman Eve said to the Lord:

> "The serpent beguiled me, and I did eat."

And the LORD God said unto the serpent:

> *"Because you have done this, allowing yourself to be a conduit for the devil, you art cursed above all cattle, and above every beast of the field; upon your belly shall be your movement of transportation and dust shall you eat all the days of thy life."*

And the LORD God said unto the Satan, the devil, the fallen archangel:

> *"And I will put enmity between you and the woman, and between your seed and her seed; it shall bruise your head, and you shall bruise his heel."*

And the LORD said unto the woman Eve:

> *"I will greatly multiply your sorrow and your conception; in sorrow and pain you shall bring forth children; and your desire shall be to your husband as one that leads you, and he shall rule, and be the head over you."*

And unto Adam the Lord said:

> *"Because you have hearkened unto the voice of your wife, and not me, and have eaten of the tree, of which I commanded you, saying, 'you shall not eat of it'."*

> *"Cursed is the ground of the earth for your sake; and in sorrow shall you eat of*

it all the days of thy life. Thorns also and thistles shall it bring forth to you; and you shall eat the herb of the field."

"In the sweat of your face shall you eat bread, until you return unto the ground; for out of the ground were you taken and formed. For from the dust you are, and unto dust shall you return."

Because, Lord God requires a blood sacrifice for the punishment of sin, He killed and sacrificed chosen beast of the field to make coats of skins, and clothed the man Adam and his wife Eve.

And the Lord God said to *his Father self, his Holy Spirit self, and his Wisdom Word self*:

"Behold, the man is become as one of us, to know good and evil: and now, before he put forth his hand, and take also of the "Tree of Life" in the midst of the garden, and eat, and live forever in sin; we must remove him from the garden."

Therefore the Lord God sent angels into the earth, eastward in Eden to the special garden with the purpose to drive out both the man Adam and his wife Eve from the garden; based on the sentence of punishment from the Lord.

So the Lord God sent angels and drove out the man from the garden; and he placed at the east entrance of the garden of Eden Cherubim, and a flaming sword which turned every way, to protect of the "Tree of Life" and preventing the man from being able to return back into the garden again!

When I, Enoch realized that being a man and a descent of Adam that being in his bloodline I was held accountable for the sin of Adam; although I did not sin like Adam.

I, Enoch therefore, ask the Lord God this question about sin, Eve and her nature, seeing that God knows the future from the beginning.

> "Great Lord and all knowing God of great mercy, what then was Eve's original penalty, and why did you create her knowing that she would sin and place her in the garden, when you saw the end from the beginning?"

Then God answered me saying:

> *"For Eve was created so that if man in his own free will chose to sin, and the penalty of sin is death, one can then be saved by the other."*

> *"Thus, Adam would be saved from the Lake of Fire reserved for Satan and his host of followers; for this Lake of Fire was not made for Adam and his descendents."*

> *"By giving man a male and female nature, I have provided an escape for man and a way for him to live in my presence for eternity."*

"For the angels are not male and female but are of a single nature being first created on the second day; and of a fixed number I made the angels."

"And look Enoch, your mother Eve has fulfilled my intuitions; therefore Enoch in the second coming, the Son of Man, the seed of the woman, whose name will be Jesus, will come."

"In the fulfillment of that day, I will have put an end to all sin; and you and your descendents will be saved forever and live for an eternity, in places of paradise, even within the Holy Courtyards of the Lord."

And I, Enoch wrote down all that I was commanded saw, and heard.

1.10 The Names of the Dimensions of Heaven

I Enoch was caught up in a vision and summoned into Heaven where God showed me of his wisdom and power, and how he created the various dimensions of the heavens, earthly forces, and all moving things, even down to man.

And, I Enoch was guided by the angels of heaven on a trip through the heavens to be a witness to the various dimensions of the heavens; where I was eventually led to the Throne of God. There different angels led me on a tour to the different locations, showing me the great sites and wonders that exist in those heavens.

I was commanded to write down all that I saw and heard, about the various dimensions of the heavens in great detail, or as much as the Spirit allowed me to recall, and to write down.

It was shown and revealed to me Enoch that the Universe is made of seven (7) dimensions of the heavens that are earth like is some respects. And there are three (3) holy court dimensions of the heavens. And the Throne of God is in the Holy of the Holiest courts.

And the archangel angels of God lead me through the various earths like heavens, where the first heaven is named **"Shamayim."** The second heaven is named **"Raquia."** Heaven. The third heaven is named **"Shehaqim."** The fourth heaven is named **"Machanon."** The fifth heaven is named **"Mathey."**

The sixth heaven is named "**Zebul**." And the seventh heaven is named "**Araboth**."

And the archangel angels of God lead through the Holy Courts of heaven. The eighth heaven is named the "**Outer Court**." The ninth heaven is named the "**Inner Court**." And the tenth heaven is named the "**Holy of Holies**." The "Holy of Holies" is the place where I was eventually escorted before the throne of God to see the Lord's face.

And I saw the "Eighth Heaven", which is called the Holy Outer Court; there I saw a great sanctuary, a purifying place, a changer of the seasons, and the holy host singing of justification, which is above the seventh Heaven.

And I saw the "Ninth Heaven", which is called the Holy Inner Court; and is a place of the soles of God's feet, there petitions are made by all of God's creatures.

On the "Tenth Heaven", which is called The Holy of Holies is where I saw the appearance of the Lord's Throne. And is the place where the archangel Gabriel led me to before the Lord's face.

1.11 The First (1st) Dimension of Heaven (Shamayim)

I Enoch was caught up in a vision and summoned into Heaven where God showed me of his wisdom and power, and the wonders of the First (1st) Heaven, and called it **Shamayim**.

The angels of the Lord then took me, and led me away from the Throne of the Lord on the "Tenth Heaven", to begin a trip through the lower dimensions of the heavens, when I was caught up like a leaf in the wind, in a spiraling vortex portal, and we ended up in the "First Heaven."

And the holy angels were with me, when the archangel Pravuil took me to a specific location on to the "First Heaven" a place that reminded me of the earth.

The "First Heaven" is the lowest of the seven heavens in ranking order, and is closest to Earth, and man. The "First Heaven" is a place that sits above the earth, and is above the solar system, and is above all stars, and is above all the galaxies in the sky above.

The "First Heaven" is the home to the watcher angles. And these watcher angels are at work throughout this heaven working monitoring stations, and control stations; and this place is the testing ground that the Lord designed for determining physical things that happen in the earth, the stars, and the galaxies in the skies above the earth.

And the archangel Pravuil took me Enoch around various locations and, I saw a very great sea, greater and purer than the earthly seas.

The "First Heaven" is the home to two hundred watcher angels; who keep watch over mankind in the earth. And, when they wished, they appeared in the form as men; for they admired and envied the form of the being that God created called man. And because of their occupation, they could watch and see mankind continuously.

The two hundred watcher angels are the elders and rulers of the stellar orders, who rule the stars and their services to the heavens, and fly with their wings and come round all those who fly.

In the "First Heaven" there are legions of guardian angels of snow, ice, dew, and water living in this vicinity.

And from where I stood, I looked down and saw the treasure-houses of the snow, and the angels who keep their terrible store-houses, and the clouds how they are whisked about. The "First Heaven" has an atmosphere similar to the earth's climate, having clouds, winds, snow, and upper waters.

I saw the treasuries of all the winds. I saw the four winds which bear the earth and the firmament of the heaven. I saw how the Lord had furnished the whole creation of the stellar nurseries, galaxies, stars, and the planets with the winds; and the firm foundations of the earth.

The First (1st) Dimension of Heaven (Shamayim)

And I saw how the winds stretch out the vaults of heaven in the skies above the earth, and have their station between heaven and earth; and these are the pillars of the "First Heaven".

I saw the winds of the galaxies in the "First Heaven" which turn and bring the circumference of the sun and all the stars to their setting. I saw the winds on the earth carrying the clouds.

And the archangel Pravuil took me to the living waters, and to the fire of the west, which receives every setting of the sun. And I came to a river of fire in which the fire flows like water and discharges itself into the great sea towards the west.

I saw the great rivers and came to the great river and to the great darkness, and went to the place where no flesh walks. I saw the mountains of the darkness of winter, and the place where all the waters of the deep flow. I saw the mouths of all the rivers of the earth and the mouth of the deep.

And the angels brought me to the place of darkness in the "First Heaven", and to a mountain, the point of whose summit reached to the pinnacle of the "First Heaven", and there I saw the corner-stone of the earth.

There in that place are also two hundred angels guarding the treasure-houses of these things, and the spiraling vortex portals, and how they are made to shut and open. And, when they wished, they also appeared in the form as men; for they likewise admired and envied the form of the being that God created called man. For they could watch and see mankind continuously.

And I saw the places of the luminaries and the treasuries of the stars and their birth places. And I heard the thunder in the uttermost depths of those places. There I could see various galaxies, stars, fiery comets, asteroids, planets, and all the lightings from their collisions.

In the "First Heaven" there is a region called the "Promised Land." It is a dwelling place that God fashioned that is a land similar to the Eden, that Adam and Eve enjoyed in the earth. And there He placed palm-trees of twenty cubits and others of ten cubits, and the color of the land was seven times brighter than silver.

In that land there is the treasure-house of the dew, like oil of the olive, and the appearance of its form, as of all the flowers of the earth. In the "Promised Land" every tree bares twelve harvests each year, and they have various and diverse fruits.

There, I also saw the paths of the angels at the end of the earth in the firmament of the "First Heaven" above. And I, Enoch wrote down all that I was commanded saw, and heard.

1.12 The Second (2nd) Dimension of Heaven (Raquia)

I Enoch was caught up in a vision and summoned into Heaven where God showed me of his wisdom and power, and the wonders of the Second (2nd) Heaven, and called it **Raquia**.

Then once again with the angels, I was caught up like a leaf in the wind, and into a spiraling vortex portal, and we ended up on to the "Second Heaven." And the holy archangels Uriel, and Michael escorted me as armed guards through various horrible places on the "Second Heaven."

The angels revealed to me that the "Second Heaven" used to be a beautiful place, but the Lord God changed the design of the place, and remade it a place of darkness. On to the "Second Heaven", there is darkness, greater than any earthly darkness; and it could be called a hellish place!

As the holy archangels Uriel, and Michael escorted me through the "Second Heaven" I could see the key-holders and guardian angels of the gates of hell standing, like great serpents. These key-holders, guardian angels, which look like serpents, have faces like extinguished lamps, and their eyes full of fire, and their teeth long and sharp.

On the "Second Heaven" most but not all of the fallen angels are imprisoned there waiting final judgment in complete darkness. And these fallen angels were dark-looking, more than earthly darkness, and incessantly making weeping through all hours.

And there I saw prisoners hanging, being watched by the large serpent key-holders and guards of the gates, awaiting the great and boundless judgment. And the prisoners were being incessantly tortured.

The prisoners are God's apostates, who obeyed not God's commands, but took counsel with their own will, and turned away with the prince of the fallen angels, Satan also known as the devil; whose former name was Lucifer. For, all those who obey not God's commands, whether they be angel or mankind alike they will ultimately be fastened with chains in this pit on the "Second Heaven."

As the angels Uriel, and Michael continued to escort me like armed guards through the "Second Heaven", I could see and felt great pity for the prisoners there; and they saluted me, and said to me:

"Man of God, pray for us to the Lord"

And the angels whose names are Uriel and Michael, led me upon to the Northern side of the "Second Heaven", and showed me there a very terrible place, and there were all manner of tortures in that place.

In that terrible place there was cruel darkness and unilluminated gloom, and there is no light there. There is a murky fire that constantly flames aloft, and there is a fiery river that flows through that region. And in that whole place is everywhere fire and everywhere there is frost, ice, thirst and shivering.

And, there the bonds of the prisoners are very cruel. There the serpents like key-holder, guardian angels are fearful looking and merciless, bearing angry weapons; and they are merciless in their torture.

And I saw a deep abyss, with columns of heavenly fire. And among them I saw columns of fire fall, which were beyond measure alike towards the height and towards the depth.

And beyond that abyss I saw a place which had no firmament of the heaven above, and no firmly foundation of earth beneath it. There was no water upon the land, and no birds; but it was like a waste dump, and a horrible place.

There on the "Second Heaven", I saw seven stars like great burning mountains. And I Enoch became intrigued about those stars, and I inquired of the angels that were with me regarding them.

Then, the angel Uriel said:

> "Enoch, this place is the end of the "Second Heaven" and earth. This place has become a prison for the stars and the host of heaven that did not obey the voice of the Lord."

> "And the stars which roll over the fire are they which have transgressed the commandment of the Lord in the beginning of their rising, because they did not come forth at their appointed times; when God called them to come forth."

"And He was wroth with them, and bound them till the time when their guilt should be consummated and they have been here for many billions of years."

And the angel Uriel also said to me:

"Here in the place where these stars are above, shall stand the angels that currently reside on the "Fifth Heaven."For those angels are those who have connected themselves with the men and women of the earth."

"For the angels that shall stand here entered the earth against the will of God, and used evil spirits which assumed many different forms, which defiled all manner of mankind, by leading them astray into iniquities, wickedness, and sacrificing falsely to idols as gods."

"Here these demonic angels shall they stand after the day of the great judgment in which they shall be judged of the Lord, until they are made an end of."

Then I, Enoch said:

"Woe, woe, how very terrible is this place."

Then the angel Uriel said to me:

"This place, O Enoch, is prepared for those men and women whose names are not written in the Lamb's Book of Life."

"This place, O Enoch, is also prepared for those men and women in the earth who dishonor and choose not God. And while they were on earth practiced sin against nature, which is child-corruption after the sodomite fashion, idolatries, enchantments and devilish witchcrafts, and who boast of their wicked deeds."

"For those that are found stealing, lying, committing murder, envy, covetousness, lasciviousness, hatred; and those that dishonor their vows they made to the Lord committing adultery."

"And those who, accursed, steal the souls of men leading them into iniquity and wickedness; who, seeing the poor takes away their goods, and they themselves wax rich. Taxing the poor unjustly and injuring them for other men's gains. Who being able to satisfy the empty, made the hungering to die. Being able to clothe, stripped the naked."

"And who knew not their creator, and bowed down to soulless, lifeless, false idol gods; who cannot see or hear. Those who worship vain idol gods, whose images they built with their own hands; they bow down to an unclean handiwork."

"For all these is prepared this place among these, for an eternal inheritance."

Then I Enoch saw all the angels of punishment imprisoned abiding there and preparing all the instruments that would be used of Satan and his host of followers upon the earth.

And I asked another one of the angels Michael that seemed to be on guard, who went with me:

"For whom are they preparing these Instruments?"

And the angel Michael said unto me:

"They prepare these for the unrighteous persons, the kings and the mighty of this earth who sinned against the Lord, that they may thereby be destroyed."

And the angel Michael said further unto me:

"O' Enoch, but be aware that there shall come a day after the final Day of Judgment, the Righteous and Elect One, him they shall call Jesus. And He shall cause the house of his congregation to appear, with strength and power."

> "And when that Righteous and Elect One, him they call Jesus, shall appear, from henceforth men and angels shall be no more hindered by that evil one that they call Satan the devil."

> "And not one of these mountains in this horrible place shall stand as the earth before His Righteousness; but the hills here shall be as lakes of fire. And when that Elect One, him they call Jesus shall come, the righteous shall have complete rest from the oppression of sinners."

And I looked and turned to another part of the "Second Heaven", and saw there a deep valley with burning fire. And there they brought all the unrighteous, the kings, and the mighty which walked in the earth, and began to cast them into this deep valley to do work, building and fastening of iron chains.

And there mine eyes saw how they made these their instruments, iron chains of immeasurable weight.

And I once again asked one of the archangels of peace Michael, who went with me, saying:

> "For whom are these chains being prepared?"

And the archangel Michael said unto me:

> "These chains are being prepared for Satan the devil, and for evil men and women in the earth, and for the host of

innumerous fallen angels that went with him, as Satan was cast out of heaven. For, I saw him and his following angels fall down like lightning from heaven; by the command of the Lord God."

"These chains are being prepared for those men and women whose names are not written in the Lamb's Book of Life."

"And these chains are being prepared for that last judgment day; so that they may take these chains and cast them around those devils which are fallen angels and mankind alike. And they shall be cast into the abyss of complete condemnation."

"And they shall cover their jaws with rough stones, as the Lord God Almighty has commanded. And they shall no more afflict man upon the earth; and they shall have no more any memory of their existence, in the throne room of the Lord's heaven."

And, I Enoch asked the archangel Michael, why was this evil place created? Why would the Lord God create such a place?

And the archangel Michael said unto me:

"O Enoch this place was not originally created for mankind and the descendents of Adam, but this used to be a beautiful place."

"For the Lord transformed and re-created this place, for Satan the devil and his followers the evil angels; because they followed that devil."
"In the day that Lucifer the high praise archangels tried to rise in power to make himself a god, to rule in heaven; that the mighty Lord God who rules the heavens and the earth threw that angel down preventing him from rising in power:"

"For Lucifer became jealous and envious of the "man" being God created, who was to rule, and be worshiped, and be served by the angels."

"Lucifer understood and did not like that the Lord created a being called man which was made in time after the angels, but the Lord has chosen the man a second born creature to be above the first born angels creatures."

"Enoch, this is similar to a second born son being more favored and chosen over the first born son. This Lucifer the first born son of God did not want to be ruled by a man the second born son of God."

Being envious of the Son of Man, the archangel Lucifer said:

"What is man that the Lord is mindful of them, or what do they have that is special, that the Lord cares for them?"

"For the Lord has made them lower than the angels in essence, power, and wisdom. Yet, He has crowned them with glory and honor, subjecting all things including us angels under their feet."

And the archangel Michael said unto me:

"And when Lucifer the high praise archangel rejected the Lord's decision to serve man as a leader in heaven and on earth, he came up with a plot and a plan to gain power in heaven, with his following angels; having a desire to become a god in heaven."

"And when the Lord God became aware of Lucifer's plot and plan, He gave a command saying' Michael mount up an army of angels, and go up to battle against Lucifer; to bind with chains, him and his follower angels."

"And there was war in heaven!"

"As commanded, I the archangel Michael led the many troops of warring angels who were on the Lord's side. And we battled against the archangel Lucifer and his many troop of angels."

"And we fought the good fight, with strength and might preventing Lucifer and his many troops of warring angels with various angelic weapons and chains of fire."

"And the battle was a long hard fought battle, and I, led the angels of the Lord into a complete victory for the Lord sake, against Lucifer and his following angels, which when they were completely losing the battle; the Lord God stepped in and completely ended the angelic war in heaven."

"And the Lord God declared victory over Lucifer, at the end of the angelic war."

Then the Lord God said to Lucifer and his follower angels, which lost the battle!

"Who are you Lucifer?"

"I the Lord God, in the beginning of your creation made you special. For you Lucifer were created to be a wise archangel. I revealed secrets to you that I did not reveal to any other angel."

"For you Lucifer, you sealed up the sum, full of wisdom, and perfect in beauty. You were able to fly freely throughout the host of heaven and have been in Eden the garden of God."

"When I designed you, Lucifer, I designed you by clothing you with every precious stone; as your covering was, the sard, topaz, and the diamond, the beryl, the onyx, and the jasper, the sapphire, the emerald, and the carbuncle, and gold."

"I designed you Lucifer with the workmanship of various musical instruments, and the melodic sound of your singing voice was prepared in you in the day that you were created to lead the angels in pleasing worship. Heaven rejoiced, and I was very pleased, and enjoyed greatly your singing and worship."

"You o Lucifer were the anointed cherub that covered me; and I have created you like that. And I allowed you to walk with me upon the holy mountain of God. You were able to walk as a leader highly favored among the angels and you walked up and down in the midst of the stones of fire."

"You o Lucifer was perfect in your ways from the day that you were created, until iniquity was found in you. By the multitude of thy merchandise and your influence among the angels they have filled the midst of you with violence, and you have sinned."

"With your wisdom and with your understanding you have been able to garner riches in heaven, and you have garnered gold and silver into your treasures. And furthermore, you have been able to garner the hearts of a portion of the angels in heaven."

"By your great wisdom and by your musical seduction, you have increased your riches and influence with the angels in heaven. And your heart is lifted up because of your riches and influence among the angels."

"Therefore thus says the Lord God; because you have set your heart as the heart of God. Behold, therefore I will bring the Son of God, the angels that you were not able to seduce, and mankind that loves me; against you."

"And they shall draw their swords against the beauty of your wisdom, and they shall defile your brightness."

"The Son of God, the angels that you were not able to seduce, and mankind that loves me, shall bring you down to the pit. And you shall die the deaths of them that are slain in the midst of the seas and of fire."

"Will you Lucifer, still be able to say before him that fights against you, I am God?"

"From this day forward, you no longer shall be known as Lucifer, but shall be known as Satan the devil."

"For you shall not be known as a God, but shall be known as the enemy of the Lord God, in the hand of him that fights against you. For I have spoken it, says the Lord God."

"Therefore, Satan, I will cast you as profane out of the mountain of God. And I will destroy you, O covering cherub, from the midst of the stones of fire."

"Your heart was lifted up because of your beauty; you have corrupted your wisdom by reason of your brightness: Therefore, I will cast you to the ground. You have defiled the sanctuaries of heaven by the multitude of your iniquities."

"When, I first made known my plans to create man, and I eventually brought the man Adam that I created, and told the angels to worship the creature that I made, you refused and caused other angels to follow in your lead. This I never forgot!"

"Then by your iniquity you thought to rise above the throne of the Most High God and sit as God upon the throne of heaven."

The Second (2nd) Dimension of Heaven (Raquia)

"Therefore will I bring forth a fire from the midst of you, it shall devour you, and I will bring you to ashes upon the heavens and the earth in the sight of all them that behold you, and know of your name."

"All they that know you among the angels and mankind shall be astonished at you. You shall be a terror, and never shall you be any more for I will have you chained in the pit of hell."

And after the archangel Michael explained to me Enoch, why the "Second Heaven" was created, I longed to be out of the place, for the "Second Heaven" was a terrible and horrible place. And I, Enoch wrote down all that I was commanded, saw, and heard.

1.13 The Third (3rd) Dimension of Heaven (Shehaqim)

I Enoch was caught up in a vision and summoned into Heaven where God showed me of his wisdom and power, and the wonders of the Third (3rd) Heaven, and called it **Shehaqim**.

Once again I Enoch with the angels was caught up like a leaf in the wind, in a spiraling vortex portal, and we ended up on "Third Heaven"; and they placed me there. And the angel Raphael led me downwards, and there I saw a Garden of Paradise. And this paradise lies between the essence of corruptibility and incorruptibility.

On the "Third Heaven" I saw that there were two springs that come out of that garden of paradise, which sends forth honey and milk. And there I saw two other springs in that garden of paradise that sends forth oil and wine. And the springs they separate into four parts, and go about in a revolution with a quiet course. And the four springs go down into the Garden of Paradise, between the essence of corruptibility and in corruptibility.

And there on the "Third Heaven" in the garden of paradise there are three hundred angels very bright, who keep the garden. And with incessant sweet singing and never-silent voices, these three hundred angels serve the Lord and tend to the garden throughout all years, seasons, months, days, and hours.

The Third (3rd) Dimension of Heaven (Shehaqim)

Then the angels took me to another location in the "Third heaven", and placed me there. And the angel Raphael led me further downwards, and there I saw many beautiful trees and the produce of these places, such as never been known in the earth for goodness.

And I could smell all the sweet-flowering trees and I beheld their fruits, which were so sweet-smelling. And all the foods borne by these trees are bubbling with fragrant exhalation. In the "Third heaven" there is no unfruitful tree, and every place is blessed.

And from that location the angels took me to another place in the "Third Heaven", and the angel Raphael led me to a place where I could see seven mountains in the North-West. And in that North-West, location the angels showed me a mountain range of fire which burns day and night, where there are seven mountains of magnificent stones.

The seven magnificent stone mountains were all differing each from the other, and their stones were magnificent and beautiful. The seven stone mountains were each of a unique stone as a whole, and of glorious appearance, and each had a very beautiful exterior.

Of these seven mountains in the North-West, there were three mountains towards the west, one founded on the other. And there were three mountains towards the north, one upon the other. Around each mountain were deep rough ravines, no one of which joined with any other.

Enoch, What Does Heaven Look Like?

When I looked and saw the three mountains towards the west, one was of emerald stone, and one of pearl, and one of beautiful colored light blue diamond stone.

Then, when I looked and saw the three mountains towards the north, one was of onyx stone, and one of ruby, and one of beautiful colored pink topaz stone.

Now, the seventh mountain was in the midst of all the six, and it excelled them in height, resembling the seat of a throne. The seventh mountain looked as if it reached to heaven like the throne of God. The seventh mountain was made of alabaster, and the summit of the throne was of sapphire. And this mountain is that place where the Lord rests, when he goes up into paradise.

And there were very fragrant trees like sweet incense that encircled the throne mountain. And I saw a flaming fire.

And among the seven mountains was one particular tree such as I had never yet smelt, neither was any amongst them that exist in the earth; nor were others like it in the mountain ranges that I saw. That one particular tree had a fragrance beyond all fragrance, and its leaves, and blooms, and wood, appeared that it would never ever wither!

The holy angel Raphael revealed unto me Enoch, that the name of the special tree that stands in the midst of the trees around the mountains, and which stands out among the other trees is called the "Tree of Life."

And this "Tree of Life" is of ineffable goodness and fragrance, and adorned more than every existing thing. And on all sides of the "Tree of Life" and roundabout on the ground, the form is gold-looking, and like vermilion which is an opaque orange and red pigment, similar to scarlet, and is fire-like.

And this "Tree of Life" has produce of a plenteous fruit. And its fruit is beautiful, and its fruit resembles the dates of a palm. Its roots extend from the Garden of Paradise to the earth's end.

Then I said to one of the angels that were with me:

> "How beautiful is this "Tree of Life", and fragrant, and its leaves are beautiful, and its blooms very delightful in appearance."

Then, answered the archangel Raphael, one of the holy and honored angels who was with me; and was one of their leaders. And the angel Raphael said unto me:

> "Enoch, why do you ask me about the fragrance of the "Tree of Life"? And why do you wish to learn the truth?"

Then I Enoch answered Raphael saying:

> "I wish to know about everything in this glorious place. And I wish to know about the Lord the creator of heaven and earth. But right now I especially want to know everything about this "Tree of Life"; for I am being overwhelmed by it appearance and fragrance."

And the angel Raphael answered me saying:

"This place, O Enoch, is prepared for the righteous, who endure all manner of offence from those that exasperate their souls. This high mountain which you have seen, whose summit is like the throne of God, will lead you to His Throne of Glory."

"This mountain is also a place where the Holy Great One, the Lord of Glory, the Eternal King, the Son of God, Jesus the Christ will come down from heaven. From this mountain He will descend and come down to visit the earth with glory and goodness."

"And Enoch, as for this fragrant "Tree of Life" no mortal is permitted to touch it until the great Day of Judgment; when He shall take vengeance on all and bring everything to its consummation forever."

"This "Tree of Life" it shall then be given to the righteous and the holy. Its fruit shall be for food to the elect. This "Tree of Life" shall be transplanted to the holy place, to the temple of the Lord, the Eternal King."

"This beautiful fragrant "Tree of Life" is reserved for the King of Glory who averts the eyes from iniquity, and makes righteous judgment, and gives bread to the hungering, and covers the naked with clothing."

"For it is this Jesus the Lord of Glory that will lift up the fallen, and help injured orphans, and who will walk without fault before the face of the Lord, and serve him alone."

"Enoch, this place, this mountain, and the "Tree of Life" are prepared as a place for eternal inheritance; for the righteous, and the chosen, the elect of God."

"Then shall the chosen rejoice with joy and be glad; and into this glorious and holy place shall they enter."

"And the fragrance of this "Tree of Life" shall be in their bones, and they shall live an immortal life in heaven and upon the earth."

"This long life shall be lived such as your early fathers lived in the days of Adam; but, oh so much longer!"

"And when the King of Glory comes in the Day of Judgment in their days shall no sorrow or plague, or torment or calamity touch them anymore forever."

Then, I Enoch blessed the God of Glory, the Eternal King, who hath prepared such a wonderful place and has reserved such things in heaven for the righteous of mankind.

For the Lord has created great things and has promised to give many wonderful things to those who love Him.

And beyond these mountains in the North-West is a region which extends to the end of the great earth, and there the "Third Heaven" was completed.

Then, I Enoch was led by the angels, towards the South-East of the "Third Heaven", into the midst of the mountain range and through the desert. And there I saw a wilderness and it was solitary, full of trees and plants. And water gushed forth from above the ground. Rushing like a copious watercourse which flowed towards the South-East and it caused clouds and dew to ascend on every side.

After visiting that place, then the angels led me to another place through the desert, and as I approached to the east of a mountain range, there I saw and smelt aromatic trees. I found myself exhaling the fragrance of frankincense and myrrh, and the trees were similar to the almond tree.

And beyond these aromatic trees, I went farther towards the east, and I saw another place, a valley full of water. And therein like in the north there were trees, the color of green beryl, and fragrant trees such as the mastic tree.

And on the sides of those valleys I smelled fragrant cinnamon. And beyond these I proceeded further towards to the east. And I saw other mountains, and among them were groves of trees, and there flowed forth from them sweet smelling nectar.

And beyond these mountains I saw another mountain to the South-East of the ends of the earth, where there were aloe-trees, and all the trees were full of stacte a myrrh extract, being like almond-trees.

And when this stacte fell into the fire that I saw, it burnt and smelt sweeter than any fragrant odor. And after seeing the aloe-trees and smelling these fragrant odors, I looked towards the south over the mountains I saw seven smaller mountains full of choice nard and fragrant trees and cinnamon and pepper.

And then the angels led me over the summits of all these mountains, far towards the south-east of the "Third Heaven", and passed above that which looked similar to the "Red" sea upon the earth, and we went far from it, and passed over beyond the angel that guarded that place whose name is Zotiel.

And the angel Raphael led me to the Garden of Righteousness. In that location and from afar off I could see more trees more numerous than what I saw in the north-west.

Among all these trees in the south-east, I saw three great trees there, very great, beautiful, glorious, and magnificent. And in the midst the two trees there was a tree named the "Tree of Knowledge"; whose holy fruit they eat and know great wisdom.

That great and wondrous "Tree of Knowledge" is in height like the fir tree, and its leaves are like those of the Carob tree. Now, the fruit of the "Tree of

Knowledge" is like the clusters of the vine, and very beautiful to look upon; and the fragrance of the tree penetrates afar.

Then I Enoch said to the angels that were with me:

> "How beautiful is the "Tree of Knowledge", and how attractive it is to look at!"

Then Raphael the holy angel, who was with me, answered me and said:

> "This is the tree of wisdom that your father Adam and your mother Eve, who came before you, have eaten, and they learned wisdom, and their eyes were opened, and they knew that they were naked; and they were driven out of the Garden of Eden that the Lord crafted."

After I Enoch spent further time gazing upon the "Tree of Knowledge" that the angels led from there, and I went to the ends of the "Third Heaven" and there I saw great beasts that were gentle and each differed from the other. And I saw birds also differing in appearance, and beauty, and voice, the one differing from the other.

And to the east of where those gentle beasts reside, I saw the ends of the "Third Heaven" and where that heaven rests. There I saw the spiraling vortex portals where that heaven opens and closes.

The Third (3rd) Dimension of Heaven (Shehaqim)

And I saw how the stars of heaven come forth, and I counted the spiraling vortex portals out of which they proceed, and wrote down all their outlets.

At the ends of the "Third Heaven" I could see and count each individual star by itself, according to their number and their names, their courses and their positions, and their times and their months, as Raphael the holy angel who was with me showed me.

And of the angels that were with me the archangel Pravuil wrote down the names of the stars explaining their operation; also their names he wrote for me, and their laws and their companies.

And from that location Raphael the holy angel took me to another place in the "Third Heaven", and there I could see a glorious city with numerous homes of heavenly mansions in the South-West. The streets of that glorious city in the south west are all of pavements of gold.

And in that South-West, location the angels showed me a mountain range full of numerous mansion homes without number in various size and splendor.

There were mansions with porches, and columns, and large rooms. And there were mansions with porches, and posts, and small rooms. And the mansions were all geometrically proportioned, and largely spaced in separation from each other throughout the various places of the large city.

And there were palm trees, and marvelous gemstones that lined the streets of the numerous mansions in the city.

Enoch, What Does Heaven Look Like?

The Third (3rd) Dimension of Heaven (Shehaqim)

And, I saw various gemstones of onyx, diamond, emeralds, rubies, sapphires, and pearls, which freely lined the gardens of the mansions throughout various places of the large city. And the city shined and glistened like a light shining upon a hill.

And Raphael the holy angel showed all things to me that exists in the "Third Heaven", and I, Enoch wrote down all that I was commanded, saw, and heard.

1.14 The Fourth (4th) Dimension of Heaven (Machanon)

I Enoch was caught up in a vision and summoned into Heaven where God showed me of his wisdom and power, and the wonders of the Fourth (4th) Heaven, and called it **Machanon**.

I Enoch with the angels was caught up like a leaf in the wind, in a spiraling vortex portal, and we ended up on the "Fourth Heaven", where there is another beautiful garden paradise whose beauty and similitude resembles that of the Garden of Eden.

Then the archangel Pravuil took me, and led me up to the pinnacle of the "Fourth Heaven", and showed me the glorious open firmament full of stars, where I could see their entire successive goings, and all the rays of the light of a great heavenly spiral galaxy, with its suns and moons.

That spiral galaxy and the orbiting motion of this great heavenly sun and moon system which rotates continuously, is like a wind going past with a very marvelous speed; and day and night they have no rest.

Its passages and returns are accompanied by four great stars, and each star has under it twenty five billion stars to the right of the sun's orbiting motion, and four stars to the left, each having under it twenty five billion stars, altogether two hundred billion stars, issuing with the great heavenly sun continually.

And by the day, there is an early morning shift of a myriad of angels which attend to this spiral galaxy system, and by night there is a late evening shift of myriads of angels which attend to it.

Then I, Enoch looked and saw other flying creatures of that great heavenly sun, whose names are Phoenixes and Chalkydri, marvelous, and wonderful, with feet and tails in the form of a lion, and a crocodile's head. And their appearance is empurpled, like the rainbow.

The size and length of the Phoenixes and Chalkydri is two hundred fifth (250) feet long, and their wings are like those of angels, except that they each have twelve (12) wings, and they attend and accompany the sun, bearing heat and cold, as it is ordered them from God.

And there are also six-winged Phoenixes and Chalkydri that are ninety five (95) feet long, which travel with the angels into the sun's corona, and into the fiery flames. There I could also see a hundred angels kindle a sun star and set it alight.

Then I Enoch heard something wonderful, when the creatures of the sun, called Phoenixes and Chalkydri broke out into song. Upon the surface of the "Fourth Heaven" this caused every bird fluttering with its wings, to rejoice at the giver of light, and every creature broke into song at the command of the Lord.

For all of the winged creatures in the firmament above and on the surface alike behaved like armed soldiers, serving the Lord, with timbrels, violins, organs, and musical instruments of various types, and with incessant voices.

The sound I heard was sweet voices, and with the sweet and incessant voice of various singing, which it is impossible to describe, and which astonishes every mind, so wonderful and marvelous is the singing of those creatures and angels; and I was delighted listening to it.

Then the angels took me, and led me to a different location on to the "Fourth Heaven", and the archangel Gabriel took me to the site of the holy city; the heavenly New Jerusalem. It is the place of the city of the Christ, the Son of God, and the Son of Man.

The city was all gold, and twelve (12) walls encircled the city. And there were twelve (12) walls inside the city. There were twelve (12) gates of great beauty in the circuit of the city; and four (4) rivers encircled it. There was a river of honey, and a river of milk, and a river of wine, and a river of oil.

On the "Fourth Heaven" I saw a new heaven and a new earth. I Enoch saw the great city, a holy city, the New Jerusalem, prepared as a bride adorned for her husband.

The city radiates with the glory of God. And the light of the city was like unto a stone most precious, even like a jasper stone, clear as crystal.

And the city had twelve walls great and high, and had twelve gates, and at the gates twelve angels that guarded the gates.

And the names written upon the gates are the names of the twelve tribes of the children of Israel.

The names of the twelve tribes of the children of Israel are written on the east three gates, on the north three gates, on the south three gates, and on the west three gates.

The names that were written on the north three gates: Reuben, Judah, and of Levi. The names that were written on the east three gates: Joseph, Benjamin, and of Dan. The names that were written south three gates: Simeon, Issachar, and of Zebulun. And the names that were written on the west three gates: Gad, Asher, and of Naphtali.

And the walls of the city had twelve foundations, and in them the names of the twelve apostles of the Lamb.

The holy city on the "Fourth Heaven" is foursquare, and the length of the city is as large as its width. And the length and the width and the height of the city are all equal. And the building of the wall of it was of jasper: and the city was pure gold, like unto clear glass.

And the foundations of the wall of the city were garnished with all manner of precious stones. The first foundation was jasper, the second, sapphire, the third, a chalcedony, and the fourth, an emerald. The fifth, sardonyx; the sixth, sard; the seventh, chrysolyte; the eighth, beryl; the ninth, a topaz; the tenth, a chrysoprasus; the eleventh, a jacinth; and the twelfth, an amethyst.

Enoch, What Does Heaven Look Like?

And the twelve gates of the city were made of pearl; every gate was solid pearl. And the streets of the Holy city were made of pure gold, like transparent glass.

And the archangel Gabriel showed me a pure river flowing with the water of life, clear as crystal, proceeding out from the throne of God and of the Lamb, of this Holy Jerusalem city. In the midst of the street of the city, and on either side of the river, there were the "Trees of life."

These beautiful "Trees of life" are similar to the "Tree of life" that I saw on the "Third Heaven" and they bare twelve manners of fruits, and yielded her fruit every month. And the leaves of the trees were for the healing of the nations.

And there shall be no more curses, because the Throne of God and of the Lamb shall be in the city, and his servants shall serve him there.

And they shall see His face; and His name shall be in their foreheads. And there shall be no night there; and they shall need no candle, neither light of the sun; for the Lord God gives them light. And they that are there shall reign forever and ever.

And I Enoch saw no temple in the holy city; for the Lord God Almighty and the Lamb of God are the temple of the city.

And the city had no need for the sun to shine over that city by day; neither any need for the moon to light the city at night. For the glory of God lights that city, and the Son of God, the Son of Man is the light of the city.

And the nations of them which are saved shall walk in the light of that city, and the chosen men and women of the earth do bring their glory and honor into that city.

And the gates of the city shall not be shut at all by day; for there shall be no night there.

And the righteous shall bring the glory and honor of the nations into the city. And there shall in no wise enter into it, anything that defiles; neither whatsoever works abomination, nor makes a lie. But only they which are written in the Lamb's book of life shall be able to enter and exit the city.

And I Enoch really enjoyed the time that I spent on the "Fourth Heaven" and I did not want to leave that glorious place. There, I magnified the Great God of heaven and earth for creating such a place! And I, wrote down all that I was commanded, saw, and heard.

1.15 The Fifth (5th) Dimension of Heaven (Mathey)

I Enoch was caught up in a vision and summoned into Heaven where God showed me of his wisdom and power, and the wonders of the Fifth (5th) Heaven, and called it **Mathey**.

I Enoch with the angels was caught up once again like a leaf in the wind, in a spiraling vortex portal, and we ended up on the "Fifth Heaven." While in that place the holy angels Uriel and Michael led me into the beautiful southern region where it is very bright and the glory of God can be found there.

In the southern regions of "Fifth Heaven" reside the ministering angels who endlessly make new, the praises of the Lord. And the songs that they sing in that place resonate with very melodic sounds.

Then the holy angels Uriel and Michael led me away from that glorious place like armed guards into the northern region of the "Fifth Heaven." There in the northern region it was a very dark and gloomy place. I saw a great void of fire and smoke, which had no firm ground above or below. In the northern region of the "Fifth Heaven" there was no praises or service to God there.

The northern region of the "Fifth Heaven" is a terrible and desolate, place where the fallen Grigori (watcher) angels are imprisoned there.

And there imprisoned, I saw two hundred angel like soldiers, called the Grigori, which are watcher angels.

And these Grigori watcher angels have the ability to take on the form of human appearance, when they desire. And they look like giant men that are twelve feet tall; being much larger in height and stature than typical human beings that walk in the earth.

There the Grigori are imprisoned, and their faces looked sad and withered, and the silence of their mouths perpetual. These Grigori watcher angels are imprisoned because they entered the earth illegally, and sinned; and also caused men and women in the earth to sin against God.

And I said to the angels Uriel and Michael who were with me:

> "Why do these angels appear as giant men? And why are these men faces melancholy and very withered, and their mouths silent?"

> "And why is there no praise and service to God in this northern region of the "Fifth Heaven', like there is in the southern region?"

And the angel Michael said to me:

> "These are the Grigori angels, who with similar actions to their brother Satan and his fallen angel compatriots; they rejected the commandment of the Lord of light."

> "And because of their disobedience they are held in this northern region of great

darkness on this "Fifth Heaven" until the great Day of Judgment of the Lord."

"For the Grigori were given charge on the "First Heaven" to watch over the earth and mankind; and to report unto the Lord the doings there."

"The two hundred Grigori were given specific commands from the Lord, to never ever, enter the earth. For Grigori are watchers, reporters, and messenger to the Lord."

"And two hundred of the Grigori disobeyed the commandment of the Lord, and broke through, and went down into the earth through a spiraling vortex portal, on the "First Heaven." And they broke through using their powers of common vows and mutual agreement."

"The two hundred Grigori angels that entered the earth illegally took possession of the bodies and spirits of the men."

"The Grigori being in possession of the bodies and spirits of man saw the daughters of men, and how beautiful they are, and took upon. And they took themselves wives having much sex with them, and befouled the earth with their innumerous evil deeds; being in fashion like men."

"And therefore God has judged them with great judgment, and they weep for each other all the day; here imprisoned in this northern region of the "Fifth Heaven." And they will be punished on the Lord's great Day of Judgment."

Now it was revealed to me Enoch that in the days when the children of men had multiplied in the earth, that in those days beautiful and comely daughters were born to the children of men. That a certain sect of the angels named the Grigori (watcher) angels entered the earth illegally against the command of the Lord.

The Grigori (watcher) angels two hundred in number were assigned to be watchers, reporters, and messenger to the Lord, about the goings of the earth, and mankind as they walked upon the face of the earth.

However these two hundred Grigori (watcher) angels were not with the group of fallen angels that were thrown out of heaven with Satan that devil.

During that great departure of the fallen angels, the Grigori (watcher) angels remained faithful in heaven serving and praising God the Lord of Glory.

But, much later in time, as the two hundred Grigori (watcher) angels were doing their assigned job watching over the earth, and mankind as they walked upon the earth; that the Grigori became jealous and envious of man, and the joy that they were experiencing in the earth.

Now the Grigori (watcher) angels, who were in the "First Heaven", doing their job watching over the earth and mankind, saw and lusted after the men and the women having fun in the earth, and said to one another:

> "Look at all of the joy, fun, and excitement that the men have in the earth. For men in the earth enjoy much partying, playing, singing, and dancing, and having sex with the daughters of men in the earth."

And Samyaza, who was the leader of the Grigori (watcher) angels, said unto the rest of the watchers:

> "Come, let us break through into the earth and through the possession of the spirits let us enter into the bodies of man; to experience joy, fun, and excitement with the men of the earth."

> "Let us all two hundred Grigori enter the earth to party, play, and to sing, and dance in the earth. And let us choose beautiful wives from among the children of men, to have sex with the daughters of men."

And Samyaza, leader of the Grigori (watcher) angels, said further unto the rest of the watchers:

> "I fear that you will not indeed agree to do this deed, because you fear the Lord. However, I am not strong enough and do not have the power to break through

into the earth, and do this alone. And if the Lord comes to know this thing, I alone shall have to pay the penalty of a great sin."

"Will not, you all join with me, and let us do this thing together?"

And all two hundred Grigori (watcher) angels answered Samyaza and said:

"Let us all two hundred in number, together swear by an oath, and all bind together by mutual accord, and power, not to abandon this plan, but to do fully do this thing!"

Then swore the two hundred Grigori all together and bound themselves by mutual agreeing and cutting of themselves and exchanging in angelic fluids; such that all would agree upon it, and not deviate.

And this mutual agreeing and binding of the two hundred would be part of their strength and power that allowed them to open the spiraling vortex portal on the "First Heaven" and break through, to enter the earth.

Then when all the Grigori (watcher) angels came together and each agreed with one accord with their power, imagination, and wills; that a portal to the earth opened up. And they were in all two hundred; who descended in the earth because they had sworn, and bound themselves by mutual agreement.

And they were in all two hundred; who descended in the days of Jared on the summit of Mount Hermon, and they called it Mount Hermon, because they had sworn and bound themselves by mutual imprecations descending upon it.

And immediately the two hundred Grigori began to choose men, and gain possession of their bodies and spirits.

Now, when these evil spirits entered into the men they began to do all sorts of evil in the earth; and they began to teach other men to do evil with their deeds.

For these men possessed with evil spirits of the Grigori angels did all kinds of revelry, iniquity, and wickedness, in the earth. And they enjoyed much partying, playing, singing, and dancing in the earth; and having much sex with the daughters of men.

And at that time these men possessed with evil spirits of the Grigori angels also produced children in the earth that were very intelligent, large in stature, and very wicked. The children of these men possessed with evil spirits of the Grigori angels became warriors; many men followed them, and they were men of renown, and famed in the earth at that time.

Now, when the Lord of Glory found out that the Grigori (watcher) angels broke into the earth illegally and against His commands through a portal; that this angered the Lord greatly.

Then, the Lord God sent the archangel Michael and other war angels of the Lord, to bind up the Grigori angels and to destroy the wicked men in the earth that the Grigori were able to take body and spirit possession of including their children.

And the archangel Michael said to me:

> "Enoch, the Grigori did not go easily, nor did they want to leave the earth; because they were enjoying themselves immensely."

> "But the Lord gave me the archangel Michael command to bind the two hundred Grigori, and to remove them from the earth. And as I and the other angels that were with me went a warring, they began to jump in the spirit, possessing one body after the other, trying to hide and disguise from being bound. And we had to destroy many men on that occasion."

And the archangel Michael and his warring angels destroyed many men and their children, and bound the Grigori. And the Lord has imprisoned them on the "Fifth Heaven" until the great Day of Judgment.

And I Enoch said to the Grigori:

> "Why do you Grigori wait, and do not serve before the Lord's face, and have not put your praises before the Lord's face, unless you anger your Lord utterly?"

> "For the Lord God has had mercy on you imprisoning you here, on the "Fifth

Heaven"; and has not sentenced you utterly to hell on the "Second Heaven" as of yet!"

And the Grigori listened to my admonition, and spoke to their ranks in the "Fifth Heaven", and lo! As I stood with those two archangels Uriel and Michael, four trumpets trumpeted together with a great sound, and the Grigori broke into song with one voice, and their voice went up before the Lord sounding pathetic and pitifully.

From that place, the two archangels Uriel and Michael escorted me Enoch, further towards the north, to another place on the "Fifth Heaven." There I saw a mountain of hard rock. And there was in the mountain three hollow places, deep and wide, and very smooth, and dark to look at.

Then I said to the angels that were with me:

"Why are these hollow places so smooth and deep and dark?"

Then one of the holy angels Uriel answered, who was with me, and said unto me:

"These hollow places have been created for this very purpose that the spirits of the souls of the dead should assemble there; yea that all the souls of the children of men should assemble here."

"This is the place where the Lord God shall separate the wheat from the tares!"

"And these places have been made to receive the souls of mankind until the day of their judgment, and their appointed time. These hollow places of assembly are reserved until the great Day of Judgment comes upon them all."

Then with surprise, I saw the spirit of a dead man speaking as if he were making a petition or a law suit. And his voice went forth throughout the "Fifth Heaven" and he made a suit of petition.

And I asked Uriel the angel who was with me, and I said unto him:

"This spirit which looks human, and makes a suit of petition, whose spirit is it? And whose voice is it that goes forth and makes petition here in this heaven?"

And the angel Uriel answered me saying:

"This is the spirit which went forth from Abel, whom his brother Cain slew. This is not Abel but the spirit that was murdered; and he represents the generations upon generations of men and women that did not see the light of the day, and were not able to be born as the children of Abel into the earth."

"Able the son of Adam was slain prematurely. And that spirit of Abel makes his suit against the evil deed of Cain who committed murder against a whole generation and a complete lineage of the descendents of Abel. And he is dedicated to doing this until the entire seed of Cain is destroyed from the face of the earth; and his seed is annihilated from among the seed of men."

Then I Enoch asked once again regarding all the hollow places:

"Why is one hollow place separated from the other?"

And holy angel Uriel answered me, and said unto me:

"These three hallow places on this "Fifth Heaven" have been made that the spirits of the dead might be separated."

"The first hallow place is such a division that has been made for the spirits of the righteous, in which there is the bright spring of water."

"This first hallow place is prepared for those men and women whose names are written in the Lamb's Book of Life."

"The second hallow place is such a division that has been reserved for the great mercy of God. Here these men had the opportunity to accept the Lord of Glory in the earth but did not; however they were not complete as fully fledged sinners.

"This second hallow place is made for sinners when they die and are buried in the earth and they were not completely retched, and judgments have not been executed on them in their lifetime."

"Here their spirits shall be set apart in this great plain until the great Day of Judgment and punishment and torment, and mercy on those who curse God, for there is retribution for their spirits and souls. There the Lord shall judge them forever."

"The third hallow place is such a division that has been made for the spirits of men who were fully fledged sinners, who were complete in all their transgressions upon the earth.

"This third hallow place is prepared for those men and women whose names are not written in the Lamb's Book of Life."

"This third hallow place is such a division reserved for the transgressors they shall be companions of: the hateful murders, serial murders, child molesters, child killers, idol worshipers, and the like. And their spirits shall be utterly moved from here to the hell of the "Second Heaven" on the Lords Day of Final Judgment."

Then I Enoch blessed the Lord of glory and said:

"Blessed be my Lord, the Lord of righteousness, who is the great judge of men and of angels, and rules for ever."

And I, Enoch wrote down all that I was commanded, saw, and heard on the dimension of the "Fifth Heaven."

1.16 The Sixth (6th) Dimension of Heaven (Zebul)

I Enoch was caught up in a vision and summoned into Heaven where God showed me of his wisdom and power, and the wonders of the Sixth (6th) Heaven, and called it **Zebul**.

I Enoch once again with the angels was caught up like a leaf in the wind, in a spiraling vortex portal, and we ended up on the "Sixth Heaven", and there the archangel Pravuil took me to a location where I saw seven bands of angels known as the "Tell All Angels."

The "Tell All Angels" are very bright and very glorious, and their faces shine more than the sun's shining and glistening. They all have similar looking faces; there is no difference in their appearance at all. Their behaviors are the same and they have the same manner of dress.

These seven bands of "Tell All Angels" that reside on the "Sixth Heaven" make the orders, and learn the goings of the various dimensions of the heavens, the galaxies, the stars; and the alteration of the moons, and the revolutions of the suns, and the good government of the creation.

The "Sixth Heaven" is like a wonderful kingdom, and is home to the heavenly Universities of knowledge and is open to all; angels and mankind. There the study of an endless array of subjects including: mathematics, astronomy, biology, genetics, ecology, geography, meteorology, sociology, the laws of nature, the ways of the angels, and all the ways of mankind are studied there.

On the "Sixth Heaven" there are many Holy libraries of the Lord, and it is the home to study knowledge, and instruction, and learning of all subjects under the heavens.

The seven bands of "Tell All Angels" which reside on the "Sixth Heaven" are expert in the understanding of all creation and the created beings of God.

These "Tell All Angels" see the good and the evil doings throughout all the dimensions of the heavens and the earth. They make recommendations, orders, and instruction, in the form of sweet and loud singing petitions. And their songs of petition and praise inform the Lord of the entire goings in the heavens and the earth.

These "Tell All Angels" that reside on the "Sixth Heaven" are high ranking among the angels, and their jobs are to record and write down about all life in the heavens and on earth. Their perpetual assignments from the Lord God are to record in the manuscripts of heaven all the deeds of the angels and of mankind; and they are stored in the holy libraries there.

On the "Sixth Heaven" there are angels that reside there who are appointed to write down and record seasons and years. There are angels that reside there who are appointed to write down and record the courses of the rivers and seas. There are angels that reside there who are appointed to write down and record the growth and production of the fruits of the earth.

There are angels that reside there who are appointed to write down and record every growth of grass, giving food to all that is to every living thing in the heavens and earth. There are angels that reside there who are appointed to write and record all the souls of men, and all their deeds, and their lives before the Lord's face.

The "Sixth Heaven" is also home to the seven two winged servant Phoenixes and the seven servant Cherubim who sing the praises of God; and carry out special request of the Lord. There is a multitude of other angelic beings that also reside here.

I Enoch saw in the center of the "Sixth Heaven" and residing in their midst of the other angels the six winged Phoenixes, and six winged Cherubim, and other six six-winged ones who continually with one voice and singing in harmony with one voice rejoice before the Lord that created the heavens and the earth.

It is not possible with adequate words to describe their wonderful and glorious singing of these choirs, it is such a soothing audible sound of melodies and harmonies; and they rejoice before the Lord at his footstool, staging choirs, musicals, and concerts before Him.

Then the archangel Pravuil took me and led me through other parts of the "Sixth Heaven" and there I saw very beautiful mountain ranges, with what appeared to be snow covered caps.

I saw various and beautiful trees of all sorts and various colors, and they were all blooming with sweet smelling fragrances, and producing various fruits of all sorts that looked lovely to eat.

All of the land in the "Sixth Heaven" is full of luscious beautiful green and blue grass. And I saw beautiful vistas of a heavenly nature, and breathtaking awe-inspiring landscapes such as never seen upon the earth.

And I saw mountains of iron, mountains of silver, mountains of copper, mountains of gold, and mountains of lead.

There I saw lots of beautiful waterfalls and lakes everywhere that filled the land. I saw lots of flowing streams throughout the land that flowed with water, milk, honey all good for the tasting.

There is an array and lots of very gently animals creatures that roam throughout the land. And I could see and hear various beautiful birds that fly throughout the land in the "Sixth Heaven"; singing very softly and making melody of beautiful sounds.

And from that location the archangel Pravuil took me to another place in the western region of "Sixth Heaven", and there I could see a glorious city with numerous homes of heavenly mansions in the west; similar to what I saw on the "Third Heaven". The streets of that glorious city are pavements of gold.

And in that west, location the angels showed me different mountain ranges full of numerous mansion homes without number in various size and splendor.

There were mansions with porches, and columns, and large rooms. And there were mansions with porches, and posts, and small rooms. And the mansions were all geometrically proportioned and largely spaced in separation from each other throughout various places of the large city.

And there were palm trees, and marvelous gemstones that lined the streets of the numerous mansions in the city. And, I saw various gemstones of onyx, diamond, emeralds, rubies, sapphires, and pearls, which freely lined the gardens of the mansions throughout various places of the large city. And the city shined and glistened like a light shining upon a hill.

The "Sixth Heaven" is created and designed by God to be a place of peace and tranquility, where the imagination, ideas, and creativity are made to flow freely and effortlessly. And I, Enoch wrote down all that I was commanded, saw, and heard while I was in that tranquil and delightful place.

1.17 The Seventh (7th) Dimension of Heaven (Araboth)

I Enoch was caught up in a vision and summoned into Heaven where God showed me of his wisdom and power, and the wonders of the Seventh (7th) Heaven, and called it **Araboth**.

Then the angels took me, once again I was caught up like a leaf in the wind, in a spiraling vortex portal, and led me up on to the "Seventh Heaven" which is the entrance to the holiest of the three (3) holy heavens.

I Enoch could see that the "Seventh Heaven" was suspended before the heavens and the earth, and is more of a large chamber passage way for the many spiraling vortex portals of heaven.

There on the "Seventh Heaven" I could see many vortex portals that led to the different dimensions of the heavens and the earth. And that heaven resembled more of an entry and exit passage way, with many stair ways that looked like ladders, and large vortex portals, than it is a place.

And as the angels led me through the passage way after them on to the "Seventh Heaven", I saw there a very great light, and fiery troops of great archangels, incorporeal forces, dominions, Orders, governments, Cherubim, Seraphim, Thrones, and many-eyed ones, and nine orders of choirs in all, like regiments; all moving in and out through this large passage, with spiraling vortex portals and stair ways. And these stair ways were long and resembled long ladders.

And I Enoch, became afraid, and began to tremble with great terror, feeling like at any moment, I could be pulled into any one of those vortex portals, and I would end up who knows where? And maybe I could not be found on the other side?

And those angels who were with me took me, and led me after them through this passage stair way and into an opening spiraling vortex portal, and said to me:

"Have courage, Enoch, do not fear."

And I Enoch was being led by the angels, and I moved toward the spiraling vortex portal and it opened up wide and pulled me through, and I entered and felt stretched and accelerated but felt no pain.

On the exit side of the spiraling vortex portal was another passage with many different stair ways that resembled ladders, which led into different parts of the earth.

And as I was allowed to move up and down any one of the stair ways, which resembled ladders, I could see men and women doing all sort of things in the earth, but they could not see me.

Then one of the angels Raphael that was with me asked me the question:

"Enoch what do you see?"

And I Enoch responded to the angel Raphael and said:

"I see men and women actively in the earth, some behaving righteously and yet some others behaving with wickedness. However, I see more wickedness than I do right doing in the earth!"

Then one of the angels Raphael responded back to me saying:

"That is also what the Lord God sees when He looks down into the earth!"

And I Enoch was able to see what the Lord God and the angels of the Lord see when they peer into the earth.

Then I was led by the angels, and we moved back toward the spiraling vortex portal and it opened up wide like as before; and it pulled me through, and I entered and felt stretched and accelerated but felt no pain. And on the exit side of the spiraling vortex portal was another passage with a stair way that led back into the "Seventh Heaven".

And I, Enoch wrote down all that I was commanded, saw, and heard on the "Seventh Heaven.

1.18 The Eight (8th) Dimension of Heaven (Holy Outer Court)

I Enoch was caught up in a vision and summoned into Heaven where God showed me of his wisdom and power, and the wonders of the **Holy Outer Court** the "Eighth Heaven."

And at one moment in my journey with the angels through the various dimensions of the heavens, I remained alone, and somewhat frightened, at the end of the "Seventh Heaven". When all of a sudden the archangel Raphael caught me up, and a second time, I was pulled into and entered a spiraling vortex portal; and as a leaf I was caught up by the wind, and I exited the spiraling vortex portal and onto the "Eighth Heaven."

And the archangel Raphael led me through the "Eighth Heaven", which is called the Holy Outer Court of the Lord. There I saw a great four walled city, and a courtyard sanctuary, a purifying place, a changer of the seasons, and the holy host of angles and mankind singing of justification. And the whole atmosphere of the city was full of the energy of life and vitality. In that place your strength felt continuously renewed.

I Enoch was amazed at the gigantic size of that Holy Outer Court city, for its size was as if the whole size of the Sun that lights the earth were laid out flat. And the entire city was very large and foursquare.

The Holy Outer Court city on the "Eighth Heaven" reminded me of the foursquare city of the "New Jerusalem" that resides on the "Fourth Heaven" but much larger in size. And there were four gates to the Holy Outer Court city, where the city of the "New Jerusalem" had twelve gates.

There were four gates at the center of each square of the Holy Outer Court foursquare city. And at the foregoing of each gate there was a spiraling vortex portal. There were four portals one for each gate.

At the entering of the gates of the Holy Outer Court there were two guardian angels that stood on guard at the entry and exit way, guarding each gate. And there was a vortex portal that was behind each of the gates.

Thus there were a total of eight guardian angels, two guarding each gate, that watched the going in and going out of the gates. At the entry and exit way of each gate, mankind and angels alike were allowed to pass freely through the gates, if their names were written in the Lamb's book of life.

Each gate was very wide and supported by four pillars with foundation footings of brass sockets. The color of the gates is best described consisting of blue, purple, scarlet and white. The colors are very welcoming, beckoning one to come inside

The Holy Outer Court served as a meeting place where God's people those living on the "Eight Heaven" and the "Ninth Heaven" would meet with the angelic priest that wear the white garments of God; and they had the task of preparing and making ready for entering into the presence of the Lord.

The streets of the Holy Outer Court city of the "Eight Heaven" are all paved golden. The four walls of the

Outer Court are tall and wide with numerous pillars of silver with bronze bases spaced with amazing geometric proportion all around; and it is truly a remarkable spectacle! The four walls that surround the Outer Court of the city are made of transparent white gold.

Within the walls of the Outer Court are giant pools of purifying water; each the size of an ocean. There are four very large pools in total around the city, and each pool is near to one of the gates.

There are various very large courtyards that are in the midst of the city, each with luscious green and blue grass that surrounds various parts of the city. And I saw lots of beautiful sweet-flowering trees, and I beheld their fruits, which were sweet-smelling, and all the foods borne by them bubbling with fragrant exhalation; similar to what I saw and smelled on the "Third heaven". And there is no unfruitful tree in Holy Outer Court of the "Eight Heaven", and every place is blessed.

And the whole ambiance of the city was full of life energy and vitality.

In the city I saw various chambers, and towering buildings with windows, and their arches, and their palm trees, which were near each wall of the four walls of the city. The streets of that glorious city are blocks of pavements of gold and there are radiant diamonds of various colors at the centers of each block of pavement.

In that four walled city the Holy Outer Court, I saw numerous mansion homes without number in various size and splendor; similar to what I saw on the "Third Heaven" and on the "Sixth Heaven". There were mansions with porches, and columns, and large rooms.

And there were mansions with porches, and posts, and small rooms. And the mansions were all geometrically proportioned and largely spaced in separation from each other throughout various places of the large city.

And there were palm trees, and marvelous gemstones that lined the streets of the numerous mansions in the city. And, I saw various gemstones of onyx, diamond, emeralds, rubies, sapphires, and pearls, which freely lined the gardens of the chambers, buildings, and mansions throughout various places of the large city. And the city shined and glistened like a light shining upon a hill.

And I Enoch after seeing this marvelous city the Holy Outer Court of the "Eight Heaven", and feeling full of life in that place I considered not going back to the earth; and I thought of the earth as a living dump, for there is no comparison with this marvelous place.

Nor did I want to write down anything because I wanted to do nothing else but enjoy the life energy and the aroma of the air of that wonderful city. But, I Enoch did as I was command and wrote down all, that I saw, and heard of the Holy Outer Court the "Eight Heaven."

1.19 The Ninth (9th) Dimension of Heaven (Holy Inner Court)

I Enoch was caught up in a vision and summoned into Heaven where God showed me of his wisdom and power, and the wonders of the **Holy Inner Court** the "Ninth Heaven."

And the archangel Phanuel led me further past the "Eight Heaven" which is the Holy Outer Court unto the "Ninth Heaven", which is called the Holy Inner Court; and is place where the soles of God's feet rest. There in the Holy Inner Court petitions are made at the feet of the Lord by all of God's creatures.

The archangel Phanuel took me up, and brought me into the Holy Inner Court, of the "Ninth Heaven", and there I saw a great house of flaming fire, the flames surrounded the walls, and its spiraling portals blazed with fire. When, behold the glory of Jehovah filled the house. And I heard one speaking unto me out of the house, saying,

> *"Enoch, this is the place of the entry way*
> *to My Throne, and the place of the soles*
> *of My feet, where I will dwell in the midst*
> *of the angels and of the children of*
> *mankind forever."*

And I went in further until I drew near to the house which is built of crystals and surrounded by stones of fire, and once again I began to be affrighted. And I went a little further into the stones of fire and drew much closer to the porch of the large house which was built of crystals and fire.

The Ninth (9th) Dimension of Heaven (Holy Inner Court)

I saw a great house of flaming fire, and it was foursquare similar to the Holy Outer Court on the "Eight Heaven"; and there was a petitioning altar that was before the house.

Then the archangel Phanuel brought me to the porch of the house, with post made of gold. Then the archangel Phanuel led me past the porch he brought me by the steps whereby they went up to it: and there were pillars of pearls by the posts, one on this side, and another on that side. And I entered into that great house, and it was hot as fire and cold as ice; but I felt neither hot nor cold.

In the Holy Inner Court of the "Ninth Heaven" there was the place of fellowship and petition. And there is the table of shewbread that never waxes old nor need replenishing; and is also referred to as the table of God's presence. And this table of shewbread represents Jesus the Christ, the Son of God, the Son of Man who is the Bread of Life.

There is also a table of incense which is located at the north end of the Holy Inner Court, which represents the prayers and the petitions of those who call upon God with sincere prayers, and who believe in Jesus the Christ, the Son of God, the Son of Man. And the incense from this table ascends before Him, the Head of all Days as a sweet smelling fragrance.

There is also a Golden Candlestick in the Holy Inner Court which represents Jesus the Christ, the Son of God, the Son of Man who is the light of the world. For it is that light that is the truth, the life, and leads the way into eternal life, for all mankind.

And the chamber toward the north in the Holy Inner Court is for the priests, the keepers of the charge of the altar. These are the high priest angels and the high priest of the sons of mankind, which come near to the Lord to minister unto him.

And I, Enoch with a holy reverence for the Holy Inner Court of the "Ninth Heaven" wrote down all that I was commanded, saw, and heard.

1.20 The Tenth (10th) Dimension of Heaven (Holy of Holies)

I Enoch was caught up in a vision and summoned into Heaven where God showed me of his wisdom and power, and the wonders of the **Holy of Holies** the "Tenth Heaven."

And like being in a vision of clouds the archangel Gabriel summoned me from the "Ninth Heaven", and the course of the stars and the lightings hastened, and the winds caused me to fly and lifted me upward, and bore me into the "Tenth Heaven."

And as the archangel Gabriel lifted me onto the "Tenth Heaven", there I could see that the Holy of the Holiest, the Lord of Lord dwells there. The "Tenth Heaven", is the place of the Throne of the Lord God, who is the creator of the heavens and the earth.

And I saw, there was a great structure a second house, greater than the former house on the "Ninth Heaven", and the entire portal stood open before me, and it was built of crystals and surrounded by stones and flames of fire.

And I went into the stones of fire and drew near to the large house which was built of crystals and flames of fire. And I entered into that house, and it was hot as fire and cold as ice; yet I felt neither hot nor cold.

And all of a sudden fear covered me, and trembling came upon me, and I began to be frightened; and as I quaked and trembled within, I fell upon my face giving glory and honor to the Most High God, with repetition saying:

> "Holy, Holy, Holy is the mighty God of all creation."

And in every respect the great structure of the second house so excelled in splendor and magnificence and extent than the first house of the Holy Inner Court the "Ninth Heaven" that I cannot describe to you its splendor and its extent with excellent words.

And I saw there that great house as it were a great structure built of crystals and of flames of fire. And between those crystals there were stones of living fire; and between them were fiery cherubim, and the structure was clear as water.

The structural pillars which girt that house of fire were of solid gold, and on its four sides round about were streams full of living fire, and they also girt that house.

The walls of the house were tessellated and made of crystals, and its groundwork was of crystal. And its floored pavement was of gold and of fire, and above it were lightings and the path of the stars; and its ceiling also was flaming fire.

Looking up above I could see the chambers of all the stars, and all the luminaries. Its ceiling was like the path of the stars and of lightings.

And I saw angels who could not be counted for the number. There were thousands, and ten thousand times hundreds of thousand angels, encircling that house.

And I saw as it were a sea of glass mingled with fire: and angels are standing on the sea of glass, having the harps of God.

And I saw the holy angels of God, and they were stepping on flames of fire. Their garments were white; and their raiment and their faces shone like snow.

And I saw two streams of fire, and the light of flames of that fire shone like hyacinth flowers. And I looked and saw at the end of a walkway therein a lofty throne. The appearance of the Throne was of crystal and bright as the shining sun. And beneath there was a living creature that was round like wheel; and the Throne was above the round wheeled shaped living creature.

And I Enoch on the Holiest of Holies places, the "Tenth Heaven" there God is called Jehovah; saw the Lord God from afar at the end of a walkway, sitting on His very high Throne.

As I could see the Lord afar, there was a walkway that had the appearance of a watery sea of clear crystal as glass that could be walked upon. And along the walkway were a great number of living angels of fire aligned in the form of columns or pillars along this walkway.

And at the end of the walkway I could see three great Thrones; and they were one. One great Throne in the center slightly above the other two Thrones. The one great Throne to the right slightly below the center Throne. And the other great Throne to the Left also slightly below the center Throne. And the three thrones were altogether one great Throne.

And I saw all the heavenly troops come and stand aligned on the ten steps that were at the end of the walkway, according to their rank.

And the angels would bow down to the Lord, and would again go to their places in joy and felicity, singing songs in the boundless light with small and tender voices, gloriously serving him.

And there were cherubim and seraphim standing about the Throne. And there were the six-winged and many-eyed ones which do not depart, standing before the Lord's face doing his will. And they cover his whole throne, singing with gentle voices before the Lord's face:

> "Holy, holy, holy, is the Lord Ruler of
> Sabbath (Rest). The heavens and earth
> are full of your Glory."

And there stood round about the throne guardian angels: Seraphim, Cherubim, and Ophanin. And the most holy ones, who were near to the Holy Throne, did not leave by night nor depart from Him by day. And they never sleep, nor get tired, continuously guarding the throne of His glory.

And from underneath the throne came streams of flaming fire. And the Great God of Glory sat thereon, and His raiment shone more brightly than the sun and was whiter than any snow.

And the Lord, who is often called The Head of Days, has the image of a man having wide shoulders, and a well proportioned torso, and thick loins. The Lord, He has strong arms, and powerful legs. His raiment indescribable, His head and face like burnt amber bronze. His hairs were white like pure wool, as white as snow; and his eyes were as a flame of fire; and his feet like unto fine brass, as if they burned in a furnace; and his voice as the sound of many waters; and his countenance was as the sun shines in his strength.

And He that sat on the Throne was to look upon like a jasper stone and a sard stone. And I saw as the color of burnt amber bronze, as the appearance of fire round about within it, wearing raiment that is indescribable.

From the appearance of his loins even upward, and from the appearance of his loins even downward, I saw as it were the appearance of brightness as the color of burnt amber bronze, and of fire, and He had brightness round about.

And there was the appearance of the rainbow that is in the cloud, in the day of rain, so was the appearance of the brightness round about his Throne. This was the appearance of the likeness of the Glory of the Lord; and there was a rainbow round about the Throne, in sight like unto an emerald.

And round about the Throne there were twenty four seats. And upon the seats I saw twenty four elders sitting, clothed in white raiment; and they had on their heads crowns of gold.

And out of the throne preceded lightings and thundering and voices; and there were seven lamps of fire burning before the throne, which are the seven

Spirits of God. And before the throne there was a sea of glass like unto crystal.

Because there is a flaming fire round about Him, and a great fire stood before Him, none around could draw near to Him without permission. None of the angels could approach His Throne, and none could behold His face by reason of the magnificence and His glory, without permission. And no flesh, beast, or spirit could behold, and none could draw near to Him without permission.

For the Lord God was counselor, to thousands, and ten thousand times hundreds of thousand angels that stood before Him; yet, He needed no counselor.

And the archangels that led me around the heavens: Michael, Uriel, Pravuil, Raphael, Phanuel, Gabriel, and the holy archangels of power, who go about throughout the heavens, go in and out of that house continuously. And they came forth from the Lord's house, many holy angels without number.

And He that is known as the Lord Jehovah, the Head of Days would go about His heavenly home with Michael, Uriel, Pravuil, Raphael, Phanuel, Gabriel, and thousands and ten thousands of angels without number.

And every creature which goes about in this heaven, I heard saying,

> "Blessing, and honor, and glory, and power, be unto him that sits upon the Throne and unto the lamb the Son of God forever and ever."

And the twenty four elders fell down and worshipped Him that lives forever and ever. I saw the twenty four elders fall down before Him that sat on the throne, and worship Him that lives forever and ever, and cast their crowns before the Throne, saying:

> "You are worthy, O Lord, to receive glory and honor and power. For you have created all things, and for your pleasure, and your honor, and your glory."

And I beheld, and I heard the voice of many angels round about the throne with the various beasts, and the elders; and the number of them was ten thousand times ten thousand, and thousands of thousands; Saying with a loud voice,

> "Worthy is the Lamb, the Son of God that was slain before the foundation of the world, to receive power, and riches, and wisdom, and strength, and honor, and glory, and blessings."

And in the midst of the throne, and round about beneath the throne, there was a living creature that was altogether round like a wheel, with the heads of four beasts around the circumference. And there around the ring of the circumference was full of eyes round about, before and behind.

And of the four heads of the four beasts around the circumference, the first beast was like a lion, and the second beast like a bull, and the third beast had the face of a man, and the fourth beast was like a flying eagle. And the four beasts said:

> "Holy, holy, holy, is the Lord God Almighty, which was, and is, and who lives forever."

And those four beasts had one likeness, and exist as a single circular wheel shaped creature continually give glory and honor and thanks to Him that sat on the Throne above the creature, which lives forever and ever.

And the four beasts had each of them four wings about him; and they were full of eyes round about the ring of the circumference; and they rest neither in the day nor in the night, saying:

> "Holy, holy, holy, is the Lord God Almighty, which was, and is, and who lives forever."

This living circular wheel shaped creature with four different beastly faces flies, and is the living chariot of the Lord. For I saw this creature as if it were living beneath the Throne of the Lord God, the creator of the heavens and the earth; and this circular wheel shaped creature is the living chariot of the Lord.

And as I witnessed, beneath the Throne of the Lord of Glory, behold there was that living creature which had each of the four heads of each beast set within below their own wheel when it touched the ground.

And near each beast head that was set within a wheel, they were each nearby the various cherubim that surround the Throne; one wheel by one cherub, and another wheel by another cherub.

And the appearance of the single circular wheel shaped creature with the four wheels and the four heads has the manifestation as if it was a wheel in the middle of the four wheels. There the circular shape of the wheel and the Throne of the Lord, sat above in the middle of the four wheels, and was as the color of a beryl stone.

Now as I beheld the living chariot creature of the Lord that flies, it had one likeness in the form of one wheel with his four faces round about the circumference. Once again round about the circumference of the living chariot was the face of a lion, the face of a bull, the face of a man, and the face of an eagle. They were each round about the living chariot creature.

The appearance of the wheels that each beast head was set in and their work was like unto the color of a beryl. And the four creatures had one likeness; and their appearance and their work was as it were a wheel with the Throne of the Lord above in the middle of this wheel.

The living chariot creature with the four beastly faces, each one had four wings. And the likeness of the hands of a man was under each of their wings. And their feet were straight feet; and the sole of their feet was like the sole of a calf's foot, and they sparkled like the color of burnished brass.

The living chariot creature with the four beastly faces, each one had four wings. Each beast had two wings for flying and two wings for landing. Their wings were joined one to another; and they rotated not when they darted to and fro. They went every one straight forward as they went.

Their faces; and when their wings were stretched upward when they landed; two wings of every one were joined one to another, and two covered their bodies. And when their wings were spread out above; each creature had two wings, each of which touched the wing of another, while two covered their bodies.

And when the four beasts with their individual faces let their wings touch one another; each of them moved straight ahead, without turning as they moved. And they moved every one straight forward; wherever the spirit wanted to go, that is where they went. And the living creature with the four different beastly heads flew, yet they rotated not when it darted to and fro.

In the middle of the living creatures that moved together as one creature, there was something that looked like burning coals of fire, and lights like torches that moved up and down moving to and fro among the living creatures; the fire was bright, and lightning issued from the fire.

As for the likeness of the living creatures, in the center below their was the appearance like burning coals of fire, and beneath this living chariot of the Lord, there was fire that was bright, and out of the fire went forth lightning. And the living chariot creature could accelerate; and dart to and fro, as the appearance of a flash of lightning.

And their whole body, and their backs, and their hands, and their wings, and the wheels, were full of eyes round about, even the wheels that they four had touched the ground.

When they would go about, they went upon their four sides; and they rotated not when they went. And when the living creature, that chariot of the Lord would go about and fly, the wheels were lifted up.

When the living chariot creature would go about whether it was on the ground or flying, they went upon their four sides altogether as one. And the living creature that flew, rotated not as it moved about, but to the place wherever the one of the four heads was commanded to look they all followed it; and they rotated not as they went about.

Now, at different times over the whole of the heads of the living creature there was something like a dome, shining like crystal, which was spread out above their heads. And Under the dome their wings were stretched out straight, one towards another; and each of the creatures had two wings covering its body.

When they moved, I heard the sound of their wings like the sound of mighty waters, like the thunder of the Almighty, a sound of tumult like the sound of an army; and when they stopped, they let down their wings.

And there came a voice from above the dome over their heads; when they stopped, they let down their wings. And above the dome over their heads there was the Throne of the Lord, and He that sat upon the Throne the appearance of a man above upon it.

And when the cherubim by the Throne went, the wheels went with them. And when the cherubim lifted up their wings to mount up from their place, the same wheels also turned not from beside them.

When cherubim by the Throne stood, the wheels stood; and when the wheels were lifted up, these cherubim lifted up them also; for the spirit of the living creature was in them. Then the glory of the Lord departed from off the entrance of the house, and stood over the cherubim and the living chariot creature with the four heads, and they all stood still.

Now, this completes the description of living creature that is the chariot of the Lord, and is a circular wheel shaped creature in the middle, with four beastly heads and four wheels beneath, which I saw fly; and the creature lives beneath the Throne of the Lord God the creator of heavens and earth.

When I Enoch saw the Lord fly I fell upon my face praising the Lord. And, I wrote down all that I was commanded, saw, and heard while I visited with the Holy of Holies on the "Tenth Heaven."

1.21 The Son of God the Son of Man

I Enoch was caught up in a vision and summoned into Heaven where God showed me of his wisdom and power, and revealed to me the wonders of His creation.

And while I Enoch was on the "Tenth Heaven" the archangel Gabriel walked up to me and greeted me with His voice, and said unto me, that he was given the order to reveal unto me the secret of the coming of the Son of Man who would be called Jesus, the Christ.

And the archangel Gabriel spoke unto me saying:

> "This is the revelation of the Son of God the Son of Man who is to be born in the earth. And He will be called 'Jesus' who is the Christ, and He will be born into righteousness. And righteousness abides over him forever. And the righteousness of the Almighty Lord God Jehovah, the Head of All Days forsakes him not."

> "The Son of God the Son of Man will proclaim peace in the world and throughout the heavens. For from Him has proceeded peace since the creation of the world. And so shall it be unto all mankind forever and forever."

"And the Son of God the Son of Man, He holds the scepter of righteousness that will have no end!"

"And when the Son of God takes the reins of His kingdom, all shall walk in his ways; since righteousness never forsakes Him."

"The Son of God the Son of Man will be the dwelling-places of the righteous and the chosen; and with Him their heritage. And they shall not be separated from Him forever and ever and ever."

"So there shall be length of days extended to the Son of Man for he shall live for eternity. And the righteous shall have peace and an upright way free from adversity. For all that speak in the name of that Son of God the Son of Man shall live forever and ever."

"The name of the Son of God is regarded as a 'Holy Oath' that was hidden from mankind and the angels."

"And I the archangel Gabriel made the request to the archangel Michael that he would make known unto me, the hidden name of Son of God the Son of Man. For the Lord God revealed in secret only to archangel Michael His name; because the Lord God trusted that the archangel Michael would be loyal and keep His secret."

"And I the archangel Gabriel made this request of Michael because the Lord God laid that desire upon my heart; that I might enunciate that holy name in the oath; so that all in heaven and earth might quake before His name forever."

"And I knew that speaking that name in the oath of truth; it would reveal all that was hidden from the worlds, and kept secret from the children of men and of angels."

"And this is the power of that Holy oath of truth, for it is powerful and strong. And the Lord of Glory placed this oath in the hand of Michael to keep, as a secret until it was to be revealed to the angels and to mankind"

"And these are the secrets of this oath of truth. And mankind is made strong through this oath."

"That by Him the heavens were suspended before the world was created, and He lives forever. And through the Word of his name Son of God the Son of Man whom they shall call Jesus the Christ; the earth and the mountains were founded upon the water. And by the Word of His name Jesus the secret recesses of the mountains, became beautiful waters."

"From that Holy oath the Word of God

and of truth whose name is Jesus, were founded the creation of the worlds and unto eternity creation shall remain and the power thereof He commands."

"And from that Holy oath the Word of God whose name is Jesus, the sea was created. And as its foundation He set the sand to hold back the sea against the time appointed for the end. And by His command the sea dare not pass beyond its set boundaries; from the creation of the worlds which He commands."

"And from that Holy oath the Word of God whose name is Jesus are the depths of the heavens and the earth made fast. And they abide, and stir not from their place; from the creation of the worlds which He commands."

"And from that Holy oath the Word of God whose name is Jesus the sun and moon complete their course, and deviate not from their ordinance; from the creation of the worlds which He commands."

"And from that Holy oath the Word of God whose name is Jesus the stars complete their course, and He calls them by their names, and they answer Him; from the creation of the worlds which He commands."

"And from that Holy oath the Word of God whose name is Jesus, in like manner the spirits of the water, and of the winds, and their paths from all the quarters of the earth, for even the winds obey His voice; from the creation of the world which He commands."

"And from that Holy oath the Word of God whose name is Jesus, are preserved, the voices of the thunder, and the light of the lightning. And He preserved the chambers of the hail, and the chambers of the hoarfrost, and the chambers of the mist, and the chambers of the rain, and the chambers of the dew, until He was ready to open them and let them go about; from the creation of the world which He commands."

"And all of creation believes and give thanks before the Word of God whose name is Jesus; and they glorify Him with all their power."

"For all of creation gives thanks and glorifies, and extols the name of the Son of God whose name is Jesus that lives forever and ever. For even when any created being whether it be the beasts of the field, mankind, or the angels eats the receiving of their food, it is in every act, thanksgiving to Him that provides for all."

"And when I Gabriel spoke the Holy oath and called His name "Jesus" there was great joy amongst all creation and the host of all the angels and the spirits. And they blessed and glorified and extolled; because the name of that Son of God had been revealed unto them."

"And the Son of God whose name is Jesus is worthy to sit on the throne of His glory, and the sum of judgment was given unto Him."

"And Son of God the Son of Man whose name is Jesus caused the sinners to pass away, and to be destroyed from off the face of the earth; and those who have led the world astray."

"For that Son of God the Son of Man whose name is Jesus has appeared; and has seated himself on the throne of His glory. And all evil shall pass away from before His face. And the word of that Son of Man shall go forth conquering; and being strong before the Lord of Spirits."

"And at the end of all days that Son of God will judge the wicked and all evil shall be fettered with chains, and they shall be bound. And in their assemblage place of destruction shall they be imprisoned. And all their works will vanish from the face of the earth; and from henceforth there shall be nothing remaining that is corruptible."

"Long ago God spoke to all the angels in sundry and various ways. And He has also promised that in last days He would speak to us by this Son of God the Son of Man, whom He appointed heir of all things. For it is through Him that He also created the heavens and the earth."

"The Son of God the Son of Man is the reflection of God's glory and the exact imprint of God's very being; and He sustains all things by his powerful word."

"When this Son of God makes purification for sins upon the earth, He shall sit down at the right hand of the Majesty on high, having become much more superior than the angels, as the name He has inherited which is called 'Jesus' is far more excellent than the angels."

"For the Almighty Lord God never did say to any of the angels; the words like He said to the Son of Man."

For the Almighty Lord God the Head of All Days spoke to the Son of God the Son of Man saying:

"You are my Son; today I have begotten you. I will be your Father, and you will be my Son."

"I the archangel Gabriel was there and heard when the Lord God Jehovah the Head of All Days manifested the firstborn Son of God, the Son of Man into the heavens."

For the Almighty Lord God the Head of All Days spoke to the Son of God the Son of Man saying:

"Let all of God's angels worship you forever."

When the Lord God Jehovah the Head of Days spoke to the angels, He spoke on this manner saying:

"For all you archangels are like the winds, and you host of angelic beings are my servants of flames of fire. Are not all you angel spirits in the divine service, sent to serve for the sake of those who are to inherit salvation?"

But, of the Son of God the Son of Man the Lord God Jehovah the Head of Days said:

"Your throne, O God, is forever and ever, and the righteous scepter is the scepter of your kingdom. You have loved righteousness and hated wickedness; therefore God, your God, has anointed you with the oil of gladness beyond your companions of men and angels."

"And, in the beginning, Lord, you founded the earth, and the heavens are

the work of your hands. They will perish, but you remain; they will all wear out like clothing; like a cloak you will roll them up, and like clothing they will be changed. But you are the same, and your years will never end."

But, not to one archangel, or any angelic being, or any other creature, did the Lord God the Head of Days ever say; but only to the Son of God, the Son of Man the Lord said:

"Son of Man and Lord of Righteousness, sit here at my right hand until I make your enemies a footstool for your feet!"

And I Enoch rejoiced at the revelation that the archangel Gabriel gave to me about the Son of God the Son of Man. For the archangel Gabriel instructed me that I therefore must pay greater attention to what I have heard, so that all mankind is also instructed not drift away from it.

And I Enoch was awakened from my vision, and I was brought back home in the earth, and I began to write and prophesy these words.

For if the message declared through angels was valid, and every transgression or disobedience receives a just penalty, how can we escape if we neglect so great a salvation from the Lord?

It was declared at first through the Lord, and it was attested to us by those who would hear this Son of God. Be ready for God will add His testimony to us by signs, and wonders, and various miracles, and by gifts of the Holy Spirit, distributed according to his will.

Now God did not subject the coming world, about which we are speaking, to angels. But the angels have testified asking and saying,

>"What are human beings that you Lord God are mindful of them, or mortals, that you care for them?"

>"You have made them for a little while lower than the angels; yet, you have crowned them with glory and honor, subjecting all things under their feet."

Now in subjecting all things to us, God left nothing outside of our control. As it is, we do not yet see everything that is in subjection to us.

But we should look for this Son of God the Son of Man, who for a little while was made lower than the angels. But He shall be crowned with glory and honor because of the suffering of death, so that by the grace of God he might taste death for everyone. And so doing He will make it possible for mankind to live forever into eternity.

And I, Enoch wrote down all that I was commanded, saw, and heard when I was summoned into heaven by the Lord God Almighty, the Head and the End of All Days.

General References

[1]	Nelson Regency, A Regency Bible from Thomas Nelson Publishers Inc., 1990; King James Version (KJV) *Genesis – Chapters 1 - 6; pp.1 - 8*
[2]	Nelson Regency, A Regency Bible from Thomas Nelson Publishers Inc., 1990; King James Version (KJV) • *Ezekiel – Chapter 1:1 - 28; pp.1035 - 1036* • *Ezekiel – Chapter 10:1 - 22; pp.1045 - 1046* • *Ezekiel – Chapter 16:6 - 17; pp.1052* • *Ezekiel – Chapter 28:11 - 21; pp.1074* • *Ezekiel – Chapter 40:1 - 49; pp.1092 - 1095*
[3]	Nelson Regency, A Regency Bible from Thomas Nelson Publishers Inc., 1990; King James Version (KJV) • *Revelation – Chapters 1:14 - 16; pp.1545* • *Revelation –Chapters 4:1-11; pp.1547-1548* • *Revelation – Chapters 20:15; pp.1564* • *Revelation–Chapters 21:1-27; pp.1564-1565* • *Revelation–Chapters 22:1-6; pp.1565*
[4]	Nelson Regency, A Regency Bible from Thomas Nelson Publishers Inc., 1990; King James Version (KJV) • *Hebrews – Chapters 1:1 - 14; pp.1506* • *Hebrews –Chapters 2:1-10; pp.1506 - 1507*

[5]	Nelson Regency, A Regency Bible from Thomas Nelson Publishers Inc., 1990; King James Version (KJV)
	• *John – Chapters 14:2; pp.1350*
[6]	George W.E. Nickelsburg, 1 Enoch: A Commentary (Minneapolis: Fortress Press, 2001) ISBN 0-8006-6074-9
[7]	Matthew Black (with James C. VanderKam). The Book of Enoch; or, 1 Enoch (Leiden: Brill, 1985) ISBN 90-04-07100-8
[8]	R.H. Charles, [1917]. The Book of Enoch; http://www.sacred-texts.com/bib/boe/boe004.htm :sacred-texts.com; Evinity Publishing Inc; 1.0 edition (February 9, 2010) Amazon Digital Services - ISBN: 1420930451

Front Cover Image Credit:

Elijah and Enoch (ancestor of Noah) - an icon 17th cent., Historic Museum in Sanok, Poland

Detailed References by Chapter

Chapter #	Chapter Name & Reference
1.1	**God tells the Creation Story to Enoch**
	• *Bible - Genesis – Chapters 1: 1 - 5* • *Bible - Genesis – Chapters 5: 1 – 24* • *Bible - Ezekiel – Chapter 1:1 - 28* • *Book of Enoch – Chapters 25 - 27*
1.2	**The First Day of Creation**
	• *Bible - Genesis – Chapters 1: 1 - 5*
1.3	**The Second Day of Creation**
	• *Bible - Genesis – Chapters 1: 6 - 8*
1.4	**The Third Day of Creation**
	• *Bible - Genesis – Chapters 1: 9 - 13*
1.5	**The Fourth Day of Creation**
	• *Bible - Genesis – Chapters 1: 14 - 19*
1.6	**The Fifth Day of Creation**
	• *Bible - Genesis – Chapters 1: 20 - 23*
1.7	**The Sixth Day of Creation**
	• *Bible - Genesis – Chapters 1: 24 - 31*

Chapter #	Chapter Name & Reference
1.8	*The Seventh Day of Creation*
	• *Bible - Genesis – Chapters 2: 1 - 25*
1.9	*The Fall of Man and the Earthly Creation*
	• *Bible - Genesis – Chapters 2: 7 - 25*
	• *Bible - Genesis – Chapters 3: 1 - 24*
1.10	*The Names of the Dimensions of Heaven*
	• *Bible - Ezekiel – Chapter 40:1 – 49*
	• *Book of Enoch*
1.11	*The First Dimension of Heaven (Shamayim)*
	• *Bible - Ezekiel – Chapter 1:1 - 28*
	• *Book of Enoch – Chapters 17:1 – 8*
	• *Book of Enoch – Chapters 19:1 – 5*
	• *Book of Enoch – Chapters 41:3 - 6*
1.12	*The Second Dimension of Heaven (Raquia)*
	• *Bible - Ezekiel – Chapter 16:6 - 17*
	• *Bible - Ezekiel – Chapter 28:11 – 21*
	• *Bible – Revelation – Chapters 20:15*

Chapter #	Chapter Name & Reference
1.13	*The Third Dimension of Heaven (Shehaqim)*
	• *Bible - John – Chapter 14:2* • *Bible - Genesis – Chapters 2:9* • *Book of Enoch – Chapters 19:7 – 10* • *Book of Enoch – Chapters 24 - 26* • *Book of Enoch – Chapters 28 - 33*
1.14	*The Fourth Dimension of Heaven (Machanon)*
	• *Bible – Revelation – Chapters 21:1-2* • *Bible – Revelation – Chapters 22:1-6*
1.15	*The Fifth Dimension of Heaven (Mathey)*
	• *Bible – Revelation – Chapters 20:15* • *Bible – Genesis – Chapters 6: 4 - 5* • *Book of Enoch – Chapters 6:1 - 8* • *Book of Enoch – Chapters 9:9 - 11* • *Book of Enoch – Chapters 19:11 - 16* • *Book of Enoch – Chapters 21:1 - 10* • *Book of Enoch – Chapters 22:1 - 14*

Chapter #	Chapter Name & Reference
1.16	**The Sixth Dimension of Heaven (Zebul)**
	• *Bible - John – Chapter 14:2* • *Book of Enoch – Chapters 40:1 – 3* • *Book of Enoch – Chapters 43:1 – 3* • *Book of Enoch – Chapters 52:1 - 2*
1.17	**The Seventh Dimension of Heaven (Araboth)**
	• *Book of Enoch – Chapters 34 - 36*
1.18	**The Eight Dimension of Heaven (Holy Outer Court)**
	• *Bible - Ezekiel – Chapter 40:1 - 49* • *Bible - John – Chapter 14:2*
1.19	**The Ninth Dimension of Heaven (Holy Inner Court)**
	• *Bible - Ezekiel – Chapter 40:1 – 49* • *Book of Enoch – Chapters 14:8 - 25*

Chapter #	Chapter Name & Reference
1.20	*The Tenth Heaven Dimension of Heaven (Holy of Holies)*
	• *Bible - Revelation – Chapters 1:14 - 16*
	• *Bible – Revelation – Chapters 4:1-11*
	• *Bible – Revelation – Chapters 5:11-14*
	• *Bible - Ezekiel – Chapter 1:1 - 28*
	• *Bible - Ezekiel – Chapter 8:2*
	• *Bible - Ezekiel – Chapter 10:1 - 22*
	• *Book of Enoch – Chapters 14:8 – 25*
	• *Book of Enoch – Chapters 46:1*
	• *Book of Enoch – Chapters 47:3 – 4*
	• *Book of Enoch – Chapters 70:1 - 12*
1.21	*The Son of God the Son of Man*
	• *Bible - Hebrews – Chapters 1:1 - 14*
	• *Bible - Hebrews –Chapters 2:1-10*
	• *Book of Enoch – Chapters 38:1 – 6*
	• *Book of Enoch – Chapters 46:2 – 8*
	• *Book of Enoch – Chapters 51:1 – 5*
	• *Book of Enoch – Chapters 69:14 – 29*
	• *Book of Enoch – Chapters 70:14 - 17*

About the Author
Robert Louis Kemp (1966 – Present)

I was born in Detroit Michigan on October 29, 1966. I grew up in Detroit until the age of ten (10) when in 1976 my family moved to Los Angeles/Compton California.

I graduated high school in summer of 1984, and three days later I enrolled in college at Tuskegee University in Tuskegee Alabama as an Electrical Engineer with a Physics Minor.

While enrolled as an Electrical Engineering Student at Tuskegee University, in March of 1988, I got the physics bug; and I started working in physics all through the summer of 1988.

Then, in the fall of 1989, I was led by the Holy Spirit within, to drop out of school for six months; thus I locked myself in a room and studied only physics and the Bible. And for a total of two years all I did was study physics and the Bible.

Those first six months eventually turned into roughly twenty one years in total.

In the fall of 1991, I was ordained as a Minister of the Gospel at Greater New Life Church in Tuskegee Alabama.

I continued studying at the university and graduated from Tuskegee with a Masters Degree in the spring of 1994.

About the Author

When I graduated from college in 1994, I started my engineering and physics career where I worked for companies such as: Jet Propulsion Laboratory, Hughes Aircraft Company, Moller International, Raytheon System Corporation, Disney Corporation, and the Northrop Grumman Corporation. For those companies I focused on aircraft system design, and radar system design.

While working as aircraft and radar systems engineer and studying physics in my spare time, I also picked up a third job and started teaching Mathematics in the year 1999 for the University of Phoenix Southern California Campus.

I continue to teach mathematics to this present day, and prior to the writing of this book I have taught at the University of Phoenix for a total of 12 years.

Then in early 2010 I wrote and published a three volume books series in physics titled: The Super Principia Mathematica – The Rage to Master Conceptual and Mathematical Physics.

I hope that the reader enjoys this work; I worked on this story for twelve years (12), I consider it a remarkable story, poetry and art. I earnestly ask that everything be read with an open mind.

For me, the Holy Scriptures and the mathematics of physics are the tools that God gave man that he may live life, understand, and describe, the great works of God's created universe.

Robert Louis Kemp
July 24, 2011

www.ingramcontent.com/pod-product-compliance
Lightning Source LLC
Chambersburg PA
CBHW031318040426
42443CB00005B/133